Surrendering to Possibilities

Life, Yoga & Business

HEATHER ROSELLE

Surrendering to Possibilities: Life, Yoga & Business

Copyright © 2023 by Heather Roselle

ISBN 978-1-7388693-3-6

*For the curious and courageous
introverts who answer
the call to share a passion
with others —from the stage,
rather than from behind the curtain.*

*Just like the lotus,
we too, have the ability
to rise from the mud,
bloom out of the darkness
and radiate into the world.*

UNKNOWN

Sections

Aspire & Inspire — 7

Explore & Expand — 29

Creativity & Craft — 103

Master & Beginner — 177

Aspire & Inspire

Reading is yoga for the mind.

UNKNOWN

Just to clarify

*The road to success is
always under construction.*

LILY TOMLIN

This book was written for individuals who have a vision to fuse a passion with a future business—but have no business education or private business experience.

These same individuals answer a call to follow an undefined path, to learn in real time, to muddle through uncertainty and arrive exactly where they need to be. While yoga is the centerpiece of this book, learning, teaching and creating are the anchors of this journey.

The content was sifted from pages of notes documenting my transition from classroom teacher to solopreneur. My success is not measured by revenue; my success is measured by degrees of contentment and satisfaction, all of which have surpassed my wildest dreams.

I've been humbled, uncertain, exhilarated and overwhelmed. Yet, my motivation to create, to teach and to connect with others remains steadfast.

Hence, this collection. For you.

To support your journey from here to there…

Why this book now

*Hold the vision,
trust the process.*

UNKNOWN

It was always my goal to document my yoga teaching journey for myself and possibly others like me on a similar journey.

After years of quietly creating classes and workshops for a small group of dedicated women and a few good men, I had an abundance of notes, papers, journals and digital files stored and saved. This abundance had become cumbersome; it was time to delete, recycle and organize it into a publication. Knowing this was to be a formidable task, I rationalized my efforts as follows:

> If I convert my notes into a published format and no one reads it, I accomplish my goal of documenting my journey from teaching in the classroom to teaching from my mat.

> If I write this and others find value or support for their journey, my learning becomes their guide.

If you are reading this page or maybe this book, I am simply grateful.

Would you

*Be fearless in the pursuit
of what sets your soul on fire.*

UNKNOWN

Invest time, energy money into a process that leads to discomfort, failure and uncertainty?

Then, continue stepping towards more discomfort trusting you will eventually arrive a place that feels like home?

This is called following your heart's calling, encouraging you to:

- Stray from the comfort of what you know.

- Step on a path paved with unprecedented struggles.

- Accept more questions than answers.

- Envision the future without turning back.

You are not alone.

There were millions before you. There will be millions more after you.

All on this pilgrimage towards authenticity.

Recall a time when you tried something new.

Something of your choosing.

Something you enjoyed and were interested in, but your abilities resulted in the very opposite of perfection!

Yet, you remained joyful, despite your performance.

Reflecting Directions

Bring yourself to your mat.

This is your boardroom, your conference room, your office and your studio.

A place to practice, to plan and to create.

I knew…

Yoga was my path to some future destination.

The more I practiced yoga, the more confident I became to change career paths.

I wanted to discover…

A classroom where all participants chose to attend the class I was teaching.

What do you know…

What do you want to discover…

Because you are not

When your paths merge,
rejoice for their presence in your life.
When the paths are separated,
return to the wholeness of yourself,
give thanks for the footprints left on your soul,
and embrace the time to journey on your own.

UNKNOWN

In the early days of transitioning from a classroom teaching career to building my small business, those days with little or no revenue, I listened for invitations to connect with others—partly because it's lonely being a solopreneur, but mostly because connecting with others injects optimism into the future.

One of the richest invitations I received was to join a group of wise women for a conversation about aging and fitness. This group was not interested in clothing sizes, body weight or outward appearances; these women aspired to age well so they could walk with their friends, enjoy the company of their grandchildren and look after family or neighbors when health issues arose.

They had witnessed, and in many cases experienced, numerous fitness trends over the years, but struggled to find time for their personal fitness. Now, at this stage of their life, fitness, maybe even yoga, needed to become a priority rather than an option—or their goal to age well would not be achieved.

While the conversation was engaging on many levels, there was a significant closing comment shared by one of the participants that inspires me to this day. She confessed, her initial response to join the conversation was to be with women she knew and trusted, but she stayed and contributed because, "Heather is not a Lululemon girl."

I most certainly was not a Lululemon girl or any other yoga girl!

I was launching a new yoga and fitness career in my fifties and here I was, standing before other women in the same age demographic, when I recognized the type of client I wanted to work with: women my own age and older.

I was inspired by the possibility that women may want to work with a teacher and a coach my own age and older!

The foundation of my business vision now had wings and the idea for this book!

Belonging to a community doesn't always mean you are the same as that community.

It means, over time, building relationships connected to that community.

I aspired to teach yoga at a time when older fitness and yoga teachers were the exception in the world of fitness.

How do your aspirations align with those you will teach?

Inspired by...

Rachel Brathen wrote a book called *Yoga Girl*. She was one of many beautiful yoga teachers building an audience of one million or more followers via social media.

Her home: Aruba.

Her yoga style: SUP (Stand Up Paddleboard) and the mat.

Looking at the photos, reading about her journey and gaining insight into her yoga thoughts was exhilarating. While I was not able to travel to Aruba or get on a SUP board, I was still inspired.

Not to be her, but to build a similar, contented, passion-focused lifestyle for myself in my home and in my life.

I wonder:

- Is there a published or social media-based yoga personality that inspires you?
- If possible, select a yoga class lead by this teacher.

As you practice, soak in the layers of inspiration from the practice.

Be inspired **by**, *not inspired* **to be like.**

Critical companion

*Vision is the art of seeing
what is invisible to others.*

UNKNOWN

Every time I started the process of converting my teaching notes into a publication, my inner critic would interrupt the process with various messages:

- You are not a celebrity.

- You do not have a social media channel with thousands of followers.

- You do not have famous yoga parents, relatives or friends.

- You have not had a traumatic, life-altering experience.

- You did not leave your worldly possessions behind and dedicate your life to those less fortunate.

- You are over the age of fifty.

- You are not a Lululemon girl, or surfer girl, or dancer girl, or Olympic girl. . .

Still, the vision remained the same:
- The pull to explore overrode the push to stay in the comfort zone.

There are thousands of nobody famous yoga teachers like me, who inspire others to get on their mats, connect with themselves and create spaces to live life within, as well as outside of, the lines.

Time to bring your critical companion out in public.

What are the words and thoughts your inner critic frequently shares with you?

How do you respond to these critical messages?

Mind-fuel

Find a space for your practice today.

Settle into your seat.

Close your eyes.

Cultivate stillness.

Cleanse your critical companion with the following pattern:

- When you exhale, recall a criticism.
- When you inhale, replace the criticism with optimism.

As an example:

- Exhale:

  You are too old to consider a career as a yoga teacher.

- Inhale:

  You are ready to explore your career as a yoga teacher.

After a few minutes, inhale and exhale only **thoughts** *and* **words** *of* **potential** *and* **optimism**.

Method-process

*True teachers use themselves
as bridges over which they invite
their students to cross.
Then, having facilitated their crossing,
joyfully collapse, encouraging
them to create bridges of their own.*

NIKOS KAZANTZAKIS

This book is written in segments, not necessarily in chronological order, from my yoga teaching journey.

Teaching, good teaching, is 90% creativity and connection; 10% curriculum. The completion of my 200-hour yoga teacher training was the beginning. The yoga sequences made beautiful sense when I was a student enrolled in the yoga training, but these sequences alone could not be the foundation of my teaching curriculum. I knew I would continually create new practices, just as I had continually created new experiences for my middle and high school students.

My journey to becoming a good teacher, first in a classroom, then from a yoga mat, is unique. Like yours will be!

Access to yoga inspiration is universal.

Converting yoga into your curriculum is individual.

All you need to do is commit to being an eternal student, thus keeping your mind open to new teaching possibilities.

Discovering your best teaching self or creating your ultimate curriculum might not be linear; mine definitely wasn't!

Which is why I've included small snapshots of my planning process throughout this book.

There are others who may not be interested in seeing my process, but if you want to have a closer look, feel free to visit my website.

If you happen to visit, remember, my plans were designed for me and my participants at a specific time in my teaching-learning process...they are not in any way, shape or form polished but you may find them interesting.

Put your memory on a *listening* channel, a channel that allows you to *hear* more subtle details...

> Think back to a class where the teacher's words and cues enriched your learning experience.

How do you think this teacher acquired this language?

Listen-Hear

Research and select a streamed yoga class, preferably a class free from advertisements.

- Set up your mat facing away from your screen.
- Participate in the practice by listening to the words only.

When the class is finished, take a moment to reflect on the teacher's language.

Did you notice:

- Unique phrasing?
- Exquisite words?
- Eloquent expressions?
- Uncommon transitions?
- Other observations?

Continue to nurture an openness for **observation** *and* **exploration!**

If only

*Better than a thousand days
of diligent study
is one day with a great teacher.*

JAPANESE PROVERB

When I started my yoga teaching journey, I wanted nothing more than to accelerate beyond feeling like a beginning teacher, to escape feeling inadequate, to run from discomfort, to enjoy connecting with those I taught.

I was so desperate to move forward, I continually searched Google, Amazon and bookstores for any yoga book to guide my transition from feeling like a student of yoga to feeling like a teacher of yoga. I found very few teaching guides, so I simply built a library of books on yoga; from traditional to contemporary and everything in between. Learning about yoga brought comfort to my ongoing studies, but did not improve my ability to teach a yoga class.

If I were starting this transition in the year 2023, I would find many more gems to supplement my teaching: books, blogs and websites. There are more yoga teacher trainings being offered today than ever before, but completing yoga teacher training or reading about teaching yoga isn't synonymous with being a good or successful yoga teacher:

> Good teaching is the exception rather than the rule—it is much more complex than it looks.

As I look back and write forward, I wonder if having access to these yoga teaching resources would have changed the teacher I am today.

I was, by no means, exceptional at yoga.

All I had was myself, my teaching experience, my love of learning and a deep-rooted call to find my ultimate space to teach.

While I continue to teach yoga from an on-line stage with a small tribe of dedicated women, I know teachers, regardless of how large or small their stage, must develop their own methods that align with their personalities and their authentic selves.

This takes time.

And practice.

Plus, more patience than you ever imagined.

The world needs more excellent teachers, more exceptional yoga teachers with a variety of teaching styles to ensure the availability of yoga practices for all interested humans living on this earth.

You have an opportunity to make a significant contribution with your emerging teaching gifts.

Good teaching happens all the time.

Just not every time.

> Can you remember someone you would call an exceptional teacher?

> Make a list of this teacher's qualities.

Don't be afraid to think outside the box of education, school or classroom.

*When you walk to the edge of all the light,
one of two things will happen –
there will be something solid
for you to stand upon,
or you will be taught to fly.*

PATRICK OVERTON

Intuition

Set up your mat space.

Take a few breaths in a position of stillness.

Allow your space, your breath and your yoga experience to be your teacher.

Then guide yourself through a short practice with whatever yoga asanas emerge from your repertoire.

As you practice, visualize your future yoga teaching self.

After your practice consider:

- What do these asanas teach?
- What can you learn from these asanas?
- How might these asanas shape the teacher you are becoming?

Embrace this unique space.

Appreciate the **teacher you are becoming.**

Explore & Expand

A writer only begins a book.
A reader finishes it.

SAMUEL JOHNSON

You and me

*If anything is worth doing,
do it with all your heart.*

BUDDHA

You may have selected this book because you want to learn more about yoga, maybe learn enough about yoga to teach others or integrate yoga into a career change or a new business. Perhaps you have completed your yoga teacher training and wonder what's next. Maybe you are simply curious for reasons of your own.

I wanted to learn more about yoga, but not on a surface level way, in a deep and significant way. Teaching was already my profession; I had been a public education teacher for eighteen years.

Initially, yoga was like an alluring foreign language. I'd only taken a handful of classes, but there was something about the practice that spoke to me. I was not physically gifted, so the advanced yoga poses often photographed would not be part of my personal practice, nor did I envision teaching others to do these magnificent poses.

The more I practiced, the more yoga whispered to me; the more it whispered, the more unsettled I became, so much so that the same question surfaced: *how could I begin such a voyage without rocking the boat I called my life?*

I fell in love with yoga in 2005.

> My first class was in an empty racquetball court at a busy fitness and racquetball club.

> The loaner mats, likely not sanitized, had seen better days.

The teacher was in her thirties, I can't remember what she looked like, but I still remember her voice.

> I felt like she was speaking directly to me and whatever she asked me to do on my mat felt so extraordinary, all my awkwardness faded.

When did you fall in love with yoga?

What are your memories of this connection?

Affinity

I adore triangle pose.

> *It brings me joy.*
>
> *It reminds me to be joyful.*
>
> *It inspires me to continually create joy.*

Think about three poses that bring you joy.

> *No matter the day, no matter your energy—doing these poses always brings you joy.*

Now, let these three poses inspire your practice.

When you finish, take note:

- How do these asanas challenge you?
- What can you still learn from these asanas?
- How might these asanas inspire those you will teach?

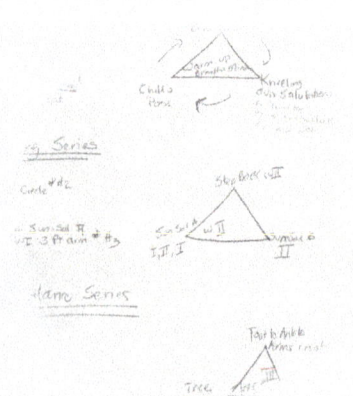

The face of yoga

Yoga is the practice
of quieting your mind.

PATANJALI

All things, over time, are subject to change—aging, evolving, adapting, reinventing. The same is very true for yoga.

Going way back to yoga's origins, the face of yoga was a man; in fact, women had limited access to ancient yoga practices. As yoga became international, it was still mostly men with some exceptions.

When yoga merged with fitness in the 20th century, particularly in North America, the shift in sex was evidenced by the faces of many, many women and a few men.

Today, yoga is continually challenged, like much of culture, to be more representative of global faces: men, women, he/she/they, children, all skin colors, various sizes, beautiful imperfections, multiple languages, marginalized perspectives and so much more!

If it's true that a picture is worth a thousand words, do a bit of research—check out the evolving covers of yoga publications, in particular, *The Yoga Journal,* from its first issue (1975) to today.

My birth year is 1961.

The images of yoga from this time are familiar to me, with a vintage hue.

> What did yoga look like the year of your birth?
>
> How is it similar to yoga today?
>
> How is it different?

Evolution

Set your timer for ten minutes.

Open your mind to simply consider:

- Yoga was:
- Yoga is:
- Yoga will be:

Close your eyes, breathe and contemplate:

- Your yoga practice was:
- Your yoga teaching practice is:
- Your yoga teaching will be:

Answers forthcoming

*Yoga is when every cell
in the body sings
the song of the soul.*

B. K. S. IYENGAR

Back in 2005, yoga teacher training was beginning to gain momentum.

As the demand for more yoga classes grew, so did the demand for yoga teachers. As more teachers completed various trainings, the demand for a standard curriculum accelerated: increase professionalism, decrease liabilities.

Today, yoga teacher training still contributes to a unified professional standard. Plus, yoga teacher training generates revenue for studios and individuals in the business of yoga.

In the early days of my yoga explorations, I contemplated becoming a yoga teacher. There were trainings available, usually long stay studies, most often requiring travel to India or Bali or other destinations.

Over time, I saw a shift: yoga teacher training needed to be more accessible and more flexible—yearlong weekend intensives looked like a possible option for me until I saw the next best thing: week-long intensives!

If I could negotiate having select weeks off work, one week at a time, I could explore taking the training one week at a time, one level at a time until I completed the requirements for RYT (Registered Yoga Teacher) of 200 hours.

It seemed safe, manageable and affordable.

If you have completed your yoga teacher training:

Why did you choose the training?

How did the training meet or exceed your expectations?

What would you do differently if you were to do it again?

If you are considering a yoga teacher training:

What are your top three considerations?

For each training consideration, analyze your investment (cost, time, travel, curriculum, instructor, etc.) using a PMI framework: Plus, Minus, Interesting.

Which training will bring you the most value?

History

Your mat is your library. Your research lab. Your sanctuary.

> *Using any form of research, dig up some yoga practices before the 1900's.*

You'll notice, historically, early yoga practices included very few asanas; those asanas included were intended to build stamina for longer meditations.

This simple practice is a stark contrast to the 2015 publication called *2100 Asanas!*

Select one historic yoga practice.

- Rewrite it.
- Practice it.

Now think back to your typical practice:

- How is it similar or different?

Your future yoga classes will be infused by the influences of the past, the present and your participants.

Because you will develop strategies for class creation, you will adapt and change with time and the needs of your future participants.

The discomfort zone

I could see in the reflection
A face staring back at me
At the moment of surrender
Of vision over visibility

U2

When change appears on my horizon, I subconsciously seek what is familiar. I was where I wanted to be personally, professionally and physically. But there was this continual invitation to learn more about yoga; it became clear that yoga would play a bigger role in my life.

To respect the will of yoga, I narrowed my options to two choices:

Just be a participant.
Take classes.
Enjoy not being the teacher.
Learn for the sake of your own yoga practice.

Become a student.
Sign up for yoga teacher training.
Learn the curriculum.
At some future time, apply this learning to your practice or share your learning by teaching yoga.

Black and white.

Simple.

Just make a choice.

The easiest and most comfortable choice was option one. This was midlife, not a midlife crisis, so why change the calm contentment in my life? I reflected on this option for a while only to realize my boat was already rocking; yoga had created new waves on the water of my life plan, ebbing and flowing in a new direction.

While yoga brought me comfort, the thought of leading a yoga class frightened me into neutral. I was petrified of speaking in public unless the audience was under the age of sixteen!

Aha.

A small, clarifying light in this tunnel of change. I was facing my biggest fear. This was the element holding me back from yoga teacher training!

This realization created an opportunity to reconsider option two; I could complete the training for myself, but then explore teaching yoga to children and teenagers. I was comfortably uncomfortable with my choice.

Little did I know just how long this tunnel of challenge and change would be!

If you are considering yoga teacher training:

    How might it augment your strengths?

    How might yoga teacher training challenge you?

If you have completed your yoga teacher training:

    How did it augment your strengths?

    How did yoga teacher training challenge you?

Silence & Surrender

Create mat space for today's *mat-spiration*.

Child's pose is a pose of surrender, of finding comfort within a practice or anytime of the day.

Work your way through this simple practice, experiencing a sense of surrender from various landmarks on your mat:

- Prone Child's Pose
- Right Side-lying Child's Pose
- Left Side-lying Child's Pose
- Supine Child's Pose
- Your Choice Child's Pose
- Finish in a Savasana Pose

All journeys present challenges...

Create **silence** *and* **surrender**
practices on a regular basis.

Tread softly

*Sometimes the strength within you
is not a big fiery flame
for all to see, it is just a tiny spark
that whispers ever so softly,
"You've got this.
Keep going."*

UNKNOWN

I completed the first intensive yoga teacher training feeling exhausted and elated. Despite all my life, teaching and learning experiences, this was by far the most uncomfortable.

The curriculum was as intriguing as I imagined it would be. I loved every moment of being taught yoga theoretically while experiencing yoga alongside exceptional teachers guiding the practice sequence with elegance and fluency, but the elements of small group and large group presenting and teaching were excruciating.

There was nowhere for me to shelter or hide.

My minimal yoga experience hindered my ability to gain confidence in the practicum teaching requirements of the course; my fear of public speaking remained ever present.

When finished, my Phase One YYT certificate in hand, I wasn't certain I would continue. My entire being craved solitude on my mat to digest all I had learned without the pressures of performing in front of strangers. But...yoga continued to call.

I still wanted to learn more.

So, I started the process of selecting dates for the second week of training. This time, the training was away from home: Nelson, British Columbia.

This curriculum was even more intriguing. Again, I loved every moment of being taught yoga theoretically and experiencing yoga with exceptional teachers guiding the sequence with elegance and fluency. The practical elements of small group and large group presentations were a bit more comfortable; I felt as though I was in the right place for the right reasons until a crisis of faith arose with one of the activities.

Without going into too much detail, the objective of the leadership activity was to find your voice. When it was your turn, you stepped in front of a small group with their backs facing you. Your task was to speak in such a way that the participants would respond to your voice by turning to face you. When the entire group was facing you, the group turned their backs and a new person stepped into the lead position.

I had my turn speaking and was now a participant with my back turned. As I had done for each of the previous students, I turned to face the speaker as soon as the speaker spoke… just as I would do if I were anywhere else. In this exercise, the activity transitioned quickly to the last participant with her back turned: it was clear, she was going to test the confidence of the speaker—his voice becoming more desperate, her stance more defiant.

I felt the shift; the exercise was no longer inspiring confidence; it was eroding confidence. I felt like a bystander witnessing the act of bullying—and I did nothing.

If I spoke up, would it interfere with my certificate?

If I said nothing, was I validating bullying?

My emotions swelled with what seemed like the memory of every child I had taught who had been taunted and tormented by bullies now swirling around me. I absolutely, uncharacteristically lost it. I left the room. I found a place outside. I had no control of the tears or of the depth of my sadness: mostly for my selfish weakness, exhibited by my choice to remain silent rather than speak up in this exercise.

As it was not my personality to be so emotional, one of the instructors found me for clarification. She was working with the other group. She listened. She understood and supported me with this simple phrase, "As teachers, we always need reminding: we must tread softly on this earth."

I was offered early completion—clearly I had met the criteria to complete the course as this was the second to the last day. But I continued…I wept through the evening practice. I wept through the morning practice on the last day.

When finished, my Phase Two YYT certificate in hand, I wasn't certain I would continue—learning the yoga curriculum was one thing, teaching yoga is a much more significant thing; something I was already privileged to do.

Of course, yoga continued to call.

I vowed to complete the third phase privately. I just wasn't sure how.

Recall a time when you had a surprise emotional, maybe even raw response...

>To someone.

>Or something.

>Or some place.

How can such responses be both clarifying and cleansing?

Restoration

All you've learned. All that is yet to come. Hold each posture for 3-5 minutes.

- **Supported Inversion**…soothe the nervous system, quiet the mind.

    Downward Facing Dog with your forehead resting on a chair.

- **Child's Pose**…invite introspection, connect with feelings.

    Child's Pose with a blanket across your back.

- **Reclining Supported Butterfly**…receive as much support as you would like to give.

    Create a reclining position for your upper body, support the sides of your knees with yoga blocks.

- **Supported Bridge**…gently open your heart.

    Place a yoga block or small bolster under the back of your pelvis, cover your upper body with a blanket.

- **Savasana**…welcome stillness in the midst of change.

    Place a blanket roll or a small bolster under your knees, cover your body with a blanket.

Ask and you shall

*What you are looking for is
not out there, it is in you.*

UNKNOWN

Once the curriculum from the second phase of training became part of my practice, my interest in teaching yoga was stronger than ever—now I was curious to explore my yoga teaching options.

All my yoga teacher employment research was consistent: a minimum of 200 hours of yoga teacher training was required by studios, fitness clubs and community associations. A partial completion, two parts out of three, would not advance my yoga teaching goal. Completing phase three of my training was not optional—how to finish was worth investigating.

The company I was studying with required participants to register for a week-long retreat: the third and final phase of the training would be experienced over six nights and seven days. Definitely not a good option for a homebody such as myself!

As more businesses started offering yoga teacher trainings, I wondered if my hours of study could be transfered. The answer surfaced immediately: it was clear I would need to either start over with a new provider or find a way to finish my 200-hour training with this group.

On-line learning was beginning to gain traction in public education. I wondered, could it also be an option for yoga teacher training?

What would be the harm in asking?

I utilized a copy of the curricular outline for phase three to create an independent course outline for my proposed on-line course completion and sent it to the principal owner for review and consideration.

Within twenty-four hours, she kindly thanked me for the ideas but declined my proposal; she felt it essential to retreat and study in person.

A day later, another owner contacted me. No surprise, she was the same instructor who supported my tearful conclusion to the second phase of training. We tweaked the outline, set dates for submission and for a final assessment... and the rest was history.

When I think back to this time, my request was out there; fast forward to 2020 when the pandemic forced all businesses to find a virtual method of doing business.

Today, there are as many on-line teacher trainings as in-person, possibly more!

A will and a way.

> When your will is strong and your mind curious, you will discover a way.

Yoga is the perfect companion for such travels.

> How has yoga strengthened your will?
>
> How has yoga showed you the way?
>
> How has yoga highlighted your unique qualities?

Receive

Find a yoga class.

Register.

Show up.

Practice by following as a perennial student of yoga.

Then, simply be grateful.

Continue to find time and space to **receive the gifts** *of* **someone else's teaching.**

Arrival-departure

*Seek the wisdom
that will untie your knot.
Seek the path that demands
your whole being.*

RUMI

A rrival:

- Yoga teacher training: complete.

- Research registration with Yoga Alliance: complete.

- Purchase liability insurance: complete.

D eparture:

- An overwhelming space to consider.

- A welcome time to pause then explore.

- A place to question where might I teach?

As there was no urgency for me to rush into teaching, I opted to explore, with as wide a lens as possible, where my future teaching spaces would be.

The obvious teaching space was evidenced with the abundance of yoga studios; it seemed like there was a yoga studio opening every week.

Rather than simply apply, I decided to select a few studios for consideration, not as future employers. As a client.

My rationale was simple: if I enjoyed taking a class in the studio, I would likely enjoy teaching a class in the studio.

The classes were large, so large that an x marked the spaces where mats would align. There was minimal space between mats; there was minimal space for the yoga teacher to navigate the room. For an introvert, this was not the space to begin my yoga teaching career.

As a newly trained yoga teacher, I had a unique vantage point. I didn't know anyone in the studio; I was much older than the other participants and the instructor; I was not able to do advanced yoga postures; I did not have the fluency to speak Sanskrit or to guide spiritual elements into the meditation or the Savasana.

To be honest, I was mostly irritated by the teaching styles—although they were all exceptional in their own unique ways and everyone else in the class exhibited contentment before, during and after the practice.

My irritation was based on what I needed to receive when I was on my mat, not what or where I was being taught.

This observation made me curious:

Was my yoga style unique to me?

Were there others craving what I was craving?

When this part of my research was complete, I confirmed:

- Yoga studios would not align with my future yoga teaching career, nor would they align with my personal practice.

The most obvious teaching location was no longer a consideration.

> **How did your yoga teacher training reshape your practice and your vision for your teaching practice?**
>
> What is the relationship between what you like to receive while practicing and how you will teach?

Challenge

Find the joy in the context of discomfort.

All yoga classes, whether you teach them or practice them, offer something to learn…

> *Especially those poses you least like to practice.*

Make a list of 3-5 asanas that challenge you.

Create a practice around these poses.

After your practice consider:

- What brings you joy on the mat will not be the same for others.

- What brings others joy on their mats may not bring you joy.

- What is challenging for you will not be challenging for others.

*You are a **yoga guide** not a yoga guru.*

Practice by creating

Success has to do with deliberate practice. Practice must be focused, determined, and in an environment where there's feedback.

MALCOLM GLADWELL

It became clear to me that teaching yoga would not happen in the immediate future. Yet, I had this unquenchable thirst to create yoga practices. I wanted to keep my yoga passion and momentum. There was no reason why my personal practices could not become my teaching practices.

I decided to design yoga practices for myself. The most natural way for me to fuse the process of practice and teaching was to treat it like an art form. What do artists use to capture their ideas?

A sketchbook! In my case, I wanted a large sketchbook. There were two advantages to this format:

- There were no lines to follow…how metaphorical, as that was exactly how I felt at this point in my journey.

- The space on the pages was vast…representing a similar outlook on what my yoga teaching practice could look like.

Perhaps this method of designing within the context of enhancing my personal yoga practice also comforted my introverted spirit. I could create without the pressure of performing. At least for the time being.

Following my instincts to utilize a sketchbook proved doubly beneficial when I did land a teaching gig—this large format functioned like a teleprompter on the floor beside my teaching space: if my nerves blocked the clarity of my teaching, I simply glanced at my page and refocused!

I love planning.

Anything: renovations, vacations, my day.

I also love the combination of planning and paper.

There is something about a pen or sharpie or pencil gliding across the page to mirror my thoughts and ideas.

Think about your style of planning or preparing:

Capture: Analog or digital?

Storage: Archive, delete or recycle?

Creations: Just words or doodles and illustrations?

Design or Default

My early practice designs were filled with notes, instructions, labels and music, all of which were to deepen my understanding of yoga and how to teach it. A plan would typically span two pages of these large sketchbooks.

My conversations with other yoga teachers revealed the full spectrum of teacher preparation ranging from *winging it* to *over designing it* and much more in between!

I suspect the style of preparation aligns closely with personality.

Whether you love spontaneity or love planning, establishing the habit of documenting your practices, before or after teaching, will be invaluable in the future.

Set up your mat and, using a writing tool of your choice, create a detailed yoga practice…either before or after you practice.

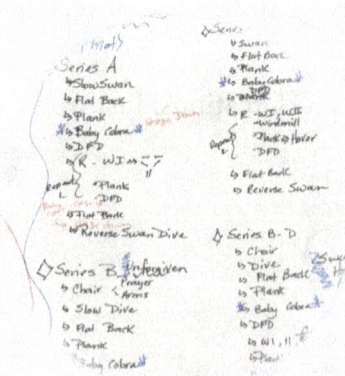

It didn't take long

The past is history.
The future is a mystery.
The present is a gift.

LISA UNGER

Although yoga classes and yoga studios were beginning to diversify, my yoga teacher training was Hatha yoga based, in practice and in theory. It didn't take me long to grow weary of the basic series of poses—my sketchbook pages of yoga practice designs started to look the same; was this a reflection projecting what my teaching practice would become? I was comfortable with the flow of the asanas, with the names of the asanas and with the sequencing of the practice, but the novelty had worn off.

It was no longer captivating or inspiring.

It was repetitive and predictable.

There are many who seek a predictable yoga sequence; they find comfort in the familiar flow of yoga postures, challenging themselves to go deeper or hold longer.

I find solace in solid foundation, but not in perpetual repetition. My public classroom practice was based on a professional promise to never teach the same lesson twice;

the curricular objectives remained the same, the content and delivery were different.

This is one of the reasons I was continually invigorated as a classroom teacher: I was learning more about teaching while the students were learning the curriculum.

Why couldn't I make the same promise to myself for my yoga teaching practice?

As I would be monitoring my effectiveness and my growth as a teacher, the sketchbook had the potential to become more than a place to capture designs. The sketchbook could document my teaching. At the end of each sketchbook, I could look back to see my progress and set new goals for my next sketchbook!

I can appreciate that not everyone would be as excited about this concept as I was, but it was exciting. A very small part of me wondered if this documentation might be helpful for other yoga teachers.

Yoga teaches us to be present, so the future possibilities of my sketchbook designs were filed away. This decision to create and document was for me, first and foremost; writing about my journey would be considered in the future.

Think back to a time when you were inspired by a teaching moment—remember, teaching isn't exclusive to a classroom.

Who was the teacher?

What were you learning?

When did this happen?

How did you feel in this moment?

Foundation

Move to your practice space.

Take a moment to record your foundation practice from your yoga teacher training or from your personal practice.

Keep it as simple as possible.

Now, do this practice.

Enjoy the sensations of knowing:

- What you are doing.
- How it feels in your body.
- The history that brought this practice to your life.

Close with gratitude.

You have a foundation
of infinite possibilities
for the future
for your practice and
for your class participants.

Where is the binder

*Creativity is inventing,
experimenting, growing,
taking risks, breaking the rules,
making mistakes and having fun.*

MARY LOU COOK

During my time as a public educator, I worked with many student teachers from the local university. Committing to excellence in teacher education, the local undergraduate education program shifted to more classroom experience and fewer theoretical courses. The thought, at the time, was there was much to be learned by being in classrooms with practicing teachers as mentors.

A young man was assigned to me for a fall semester. He arrived, interested and eager to see the school, meet some of the staff and discuss his role as a student teacher.

We reviewed timetables, routines and students. The more we talked about his teaching role, the less enthused he seemed to be.

As we neared the end of this orientation, his first short teaching assignment determined, he asked, "Where is your teaching binder?"

His perception of teaching was that courses were formatted in binders, published for and accessible to teachers:

- Select a lesson.

- Review the content.

- Then teach the class.

Excellent teaching looks that easy, but there is an entire process that happens long before the delivery to students.

I'll admit, at the early stages of my yoga teaching journey, I acquired a much better appreciation for what he was looking for.

Oh, how I wanted a yoga teaching binder!

I set myself up with this challenge to create a new practice every time, but I only had the information from my training and my limited experience on the mat!

Think of the exceptional teacher you remembered on page 25.

What might this teacher's *binder* contain?

How could the contents be organized of filed?

Imagine just how many different formats or methods could be considered!

Thinking Intervals

Find a place to set up your yoga space with something to record your thoughts in this thinking meditation.

Use a timer with gentle signals and set it for six minute intervals:

Round One: imagine the concept of your yoga binder.

- Set up a seat, use this concept as a focus for your breath work.
- When the time is up, record the ideas or thoughts that came to mind.

Round Two: imagine the concept of yoga class themes.

- Set yourself up with your feet elevated on a piece of furniture or a wall.
- When the time is up, record the ideas or thoughts that came to mind.

Round Three: imagine the concept of yoga poses as themes.

- Set yourself up in a supine position with the back of your knees supported with a blanket or bolster.
- When the time is up, record the ideas or thoughts that came to mind.

Now, look at your collection of ideas and possibilities that emerged from your thinking meditation.

This is the start of your teaching binder, disguised as a masterpiece, one that will continue to grow, evolve and mature with thought, practice and experience.

Where's the soundtrack

*Music is to the soul
what words are to the mind.*

MODEST MOUSE

My yoga sketchbook of class designs invited me to play with sequencing with a strong reliance on the principles learned from my training. I was still creating and then practicing for myself, but I knew I would need to work on my verbal cues at a later date.

I had several yoga mats I could change out; I could practice in the daylight or evening light; I could use candles; I could add props like straps or blocks, but I yearned for something else. Then I remembered one day from an early training when a yoga playlist was integrated into the practice.

Music.

The secret sauce!

This epiphany was before Apple Music, Amazon Music Prime or Spotify were on the scene. This was a time when all my CDs had been uploaded into my iTunes library; any additional music was purchased from iTunes.

Accessing music and creating playlists was already part of my home life; it was time to see how music might fit with my yoga teaching practice. My first inclination was to select yoga music, to play it safe while respectfully exploring.

If I was to create a new practice every time I taught, then I would also need to create a new playlist for the soundtrack of that practice. These, too, would need to be archived.

I have a sub-folder called: Yoga Practice Practice; this was my first attempt at creating my yoga playlist. I purchased a new age album called LagoonWest, sorted and reorganized eight songs to be the soundtrack for a 50-minute yoga class.

Music became a new source of inspiration—not in a choreographed way, just as a background to support the flow of asanas. I found comfort in a variety music genres, but I was aware my musical palate may not align with others who preferred the language of Sanskrit or the yoga-speak of gifted teachers or simply silence in between the cues.

My first playlists were not as good as my later playlists, but they all created the right soundtrack for where I was in my teaching journey. Over time, playlists became as important for my design inspiration as they were for those taking my classes.

It takes time to curate music from a variety of genres. It takes more time to place the music into a yoga playlist that aligns with the yoga practice. And it looks more professional to simply play the playlist while guiding the practice.

I have been in classes where the yoga teacher selects music throughout the practice—proving to be disruptive for both the teacher and those following.

What is your soundtrack?

Think about the sounds of your life and your preferences:

> If music is important to you, what is your budget for streaming or purchasing?

> Are you fluent in curating playlists or favorites for your library?

Remember, a playlist or a soundtrack may be musical but it can also be sounds of nature or calming background.

> Your soundtrack may simply be the silent spaces between your words.

Mood Music

Set up your practice space.

- Create a 4-6 track playlist of songs or sounds you connect with.
- Create a list of 4-6 asanas to align with this playlist.

Let the music or sound move you through a practice as the asanas emerge.

When you finish, take notes on the practice.

The pleasant.

The awkward.

The surprises.

If the playlist and your plan satisfy, save it or teach the practice to someone else.

If the playlist and your plan are not satisfactory, create another until you land on one that is!

If silence between your cues is your preference, continue to use silence as your soundtrack.

Can't you hear me knock'n

*Now, the choices you make
are not about finding your path.
Rather, they are choices to
open the path you have found.*

ILCHI LEE

Like all stages of learning, there is a time when the awkwardness of not knowing shifts towards the confidence of knowing.

It feels exquisite.

I reached a point when I realized my yoga class designs were good—not expert level, but good. My collection was growing, but the only recipient was me and my personal practice. Was it time to take my teaching outside the comfort of my home?

For an introvert, especially an introvert who avoided any form of public speaking in front of adult audiences, this created internal stress. I felt creative and comfortable, but staying home was not taking me closer to my goal: to teach yoga.

My solution was to take a few baby steps: to volunteer teach first.

When you define a path, you start to notice different signs. I'd shopped at a local Lululemon store dozens of times, but never noticed the promotion for free Sunday yoga classes.

The first time I noticed, I did nothing. The second time, I did nothing. The third time, while purchasing a few items, I asked if I could leave my name to volunteer teach some future Sunday class.

There are multiple meanings to some signs. What I didn't realize on this day was the Sunday yoga teachers were local yoga celebrities; Lululemon's ambassador program was in its infancy stage and I was not the image they were seeking. This young woman graciously gave me paper to leave my name and phone number, assuring me the store manager would contact me if there was a space to teach.

I never heard back.

I shifted my focus to the local YMCA. This organization was based on a strong volunteer program. I made contact, had an interview, filled in the paperwork, had the mandatory police check.

I never heard back.

I was an academic coach at a sports school with 400 athletes registered in the high school program. I requested permission to volunteer teach a lunchtime yoga class to student athletes once per week. I reserved an unused space, promoted the schedule, set-up for the first class...two participants showed up, but they just wanted a place to hang out and not exercise—they got enough exercise with their respective sports.

I ended the lunchtime program.

I wasn't desperate. Instead, this string of rejections oddly fortified my desire to teach yoga.

Where are your future potential teaching spaces?

List all spaces where you could teach in the future.

Expand on these possibilities with a deeper analysis using a PCP (Pros, Cons, Possibilities) chart.

Yoga Next Door

Yoga surrounds you, in both obvious and not so obvious places!

Select three unique yoga classes running on a weekly or monthly basis in your area.

For example, when I was doing this very same research, I located the following unique classes in my neighborhood:

- Yoga for Large Women
- Yoga for Stiff Men
- Yoga for Jocks

Register for the classes that interest you or that you feel comfortable attending or you are simply curious!

Take the class.

After, if you haven't already done so, add this location to your PCP (Pros, Cons, Possibilities) chart analysis.

All you need is space

*Don't think it's about
finding who you are.
Think about finding
a place where you can be who you are.*

UNKNOWN

While this chapter title sounds like a simple mantra, my search for a teaching space hit a dead-end. Next target: people not place; I would temporarily shift my focus to family and friends willing to participate in my yoga classes.

Around this time, my spouse was the captain of a firehall in an older neighborhood; his crew was small, a fine collection of three men and one woman. Could I teach his crew at the firehall on a volunteer basis?

This was a bigger ask than it may appear; most firefighters respect the directions of their senior officers. I didn't want anyone to participate as an obligation or out of respect; I wanted them to agree to my free classes because they wanted to be there.

Their answer was yes—but their preference was to have the class scheduled at the start of their first night shift. Although I didn't know this crew, I knew they did not have a lot of yoga experience. There was a shift in my preparation pattern—my focus was not what I would teach but *who*; subtle yet significant.

I didn't begin the planning for this class by sequencing yoga poses or writing a short meditation or guided Savasana. I started with a playlist...not a new age playlist! I massaged the music so it would be a distraction from the concept of yoga, ultimately creating a sense of comfort in the firehall on their mats. The mix was called *Captain's Mix*: Guns N' Roses, Aerosmith, Kid Rock and more.

The sequence was simple, a slow, basic Hatha yoga flow: short meditation, basic flow, short Savasana—forty-five minutes long, provided they were not dispatched to a call.

As the date approached, I realized the challenge: I needed to lead this class with my voice. My class sequence was good; my self-confidence was not so good.

No one was forcing me to teach yoga.

If I was going to do this, I needed to become comfortable on the stage, so to speak.

One deep breath in the parking lot and in I went—looking calm, feeling nauseous.

> **How do you cultivate courage when facing your own fears?**
>
> Think specifically about strategies you use to navigate over, under, through and around the *fear barriers*.

Plan for Courage

Set up your practice space.

Set up your system for planning.

- The more time I took to think, to consider, to sequence, to design, the more courageous I became.

As my confidence grew, so did my creativity.

Invite both courage and creativity to your class plan today:

- No sequencing rules.

- No guidelines.

- No restrictions.

What will you create?

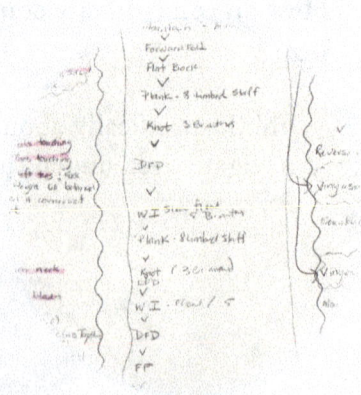

For the first time, I feel love

You are the sky.
Everything else is the weather.

PEMA CHODRON

The aesthetic of yoga studios must be acknowledged. I admire how ambiance creates atmosphere: color, wall art, fountains, flooring, upholstery.

One of my first yoga studio teaching spaces was a small room in an older firehall; the room was designated as a ping pong room. Nothing sacred here other than the potential to convert the room into a yoga space. I was comfortable moving the ping pong table. I set up the mats to ensure each participant had space to practice. These tasks temporarily calmed my nerves and settled my stomach.

Kind and gracious, the crew arrived on time at 6pm.

They patiently followed my cues, smoothing over my awkwardness by simply doing what I was asking them to do. This was *not* an exemplary class. Far from it. But the crew appreciated doing something different before a night shift. I appreciated the opportunity to volunteer teach and begin to log my public practice teaching hours.

Honestly, on this awkward first day of teaching yoga, I felt a love for teaching I had never felt. I was on the amateur end of the yoga teaching spectrum, yet energized by the possibilities and the potential for where the yoga curriculum could take me.

This taste of teaching affirmed my aspiration: this was my path.

> **Not all yoga teaching spaces are designer yoga studios.**
>
> **What can you do to create an ambiance for those you teach, regardless of:**
>
> Your location?
>
> Your budget?
>
> Your preferences?
>
> Your participants?

Mat-spirations

Set your mat up in a location least likely to be considered for practice.

Add a few simple elements:

- Essential oil diffuser
- Candle
- Eye pillow
- Something else?

Surround yourself with your senses and your imagination.

As you settle into breath-infused stillness, allow yourself to enter your mind's image of a sanctuary…using your seat, your mind and the space of time.

Stay as long as your time permits.

Finish with Child's Pose.

Surrendering to the possibilities of **your** *future.*

The language of love

The most important thing about communication is to hear what isn't being said.

PETER DRUCKER

I didn't expect teaching yoga to transform me from an introvert to an extrovert, nor did I expect experience would increase my personal comfort leading a yoga class. What I expected of myself was to be patient and refine my teaching practice through reflection, not judgement or criticism.

The reflection from my first class was simple: the concept of talking bodies through a practice felt like conversing with a mouthful of food.

My default strategy was to do the practice with them as I spoke, for my comfort, and I think, for theirs. I shifted to the easier method of providing the visual, because my verbal cues were not strong enough. I had been in those classes where I wondered if some teachers were teaching for their personal fitness or teaching to lead a practice for others.

This was not my end game—I wasn't teaching to become more fit; I wasn't teaching to become better at yoga. I was teaching to inspire others to get on their mats on a regular basis.

To honestly recognize my areas in need of fortification—improving my spoken cues, thus eliminating the need for me to practice with the participants—required deeper exploration.

There were several options to consider:

- I could improve my fluency with Sanskrit.

- I could deepen my understanding of anatomy.

- I could think of cuing like a recipe with step-by-step words for where to place hands, feet and spine.

I was not enamored with speaking Sanskrit; as beautiful as it was, I always felt it created a barrier for the less experienced yogis like myself.

I was not confident with the language of the human body, but this was an interest percolating for the future.

I could follow a recipe, so I knew I could direct simple movements and transitions on the mat, but I would need to include these in my designs. This would be another layer of information to consider while managing my stress speaking in public.

Later in my teaching practice, one of my students would call my classes *Heather says* because he so appreciated hearing where he should place his body as we moved through the class. I had become clear, organized and confident speaking the language of yoga movement.

My large sketchbook had even more value now, allowing more space for my creations.

My plans were still creative, but I was writing more, thus understanding my teaching on a different level.

Have you ever listened to yourself direct someone or tell someone how to do something?

Record it sometime—it's almost humorous how communication doesn't work until the words sent are the same as the words received!

Try doing another virtual yoga class with your back to the screen—with just words to cue your practice.

Evaluate the verbal skills of the teacher: Sanskrit, anatomy, direction, transitions or simply noting what was extraordinary and what could be improved upon.

Inspiration Sharing

Create a simple plan for someone..

Someone you know and trust to join you for a yoga practice—hopefully someone with only a little yoga experience.

Take a seat, invite your yoga guest to face away from you and deliver this plan:

- While seated.
- With your voice only.

Ask for feedback.

Share your self-reflection.

*Maximize your **learning** from your **teaching**.*

Anyone can teach

*You can buy an expensive violin,
but you can't buy ten years of practice.*

UNKNOWN

How many times have you heard someone say this chapter title? Most often, these words are spoken by those who have never taught!

It looks like something anyone can do: if you have learned something, you can teach it. Right?

This is definitely not the case. In fact, those who acquire knowledge to the point of brilliance often cannot transfer their knowledge into teachable situations for others wanting to acquire that information.

The same is true for yoga: being able to put your body into a series of advanced poses with ease and elegance doesn't mean you will be an excellent or even a good teacher—especially over the long run of a career.

So, what are the elements of teaching, yoga or otherwise, that lead to longevity and vitality in that role?

Financial motivation? Connection with others? Sharing a passion?

Something else?

There is no one answer to this question, but the answers are likely revealed somewhere in the space between what you teach and who you teach.

Content and curriculum are merely the common ground from which to begin.

Your audience or classroom is where you land.

Longevity and vitality are two elements that thrive in the context of creativity and change. While I suspect there are a few yoga class creators who fly by the seat of their pants, a lot of work happens in the space between classes.

It's called planning, the value of which is often overlooked, due largely to the scarcity of time, especially if you are teaching a number of classes a day or a week. Even if you find yoga class plans created by someone else, you still need to align the content of the plan with who you are, where you'll be teaching and who will be taking your classes.

> **Think about planning like a telescope that gives you a clear view of yoga poses.**
>
> **Then think about planning like a kaleidoscope, with a rainbow of possibilities embracing each yoga posture.**

Subtly Significant

Consider the subtle difference between doing yoga and practicing yoga.

Select your three favorite yoga poses:

- Do them in the order of your thoughts.

Then, take a moment and write these three yoga posture names on a piece of paper.

Beside each, record what you know, what you think and other ways the pose can be created…

- Now, practice these three postures with all the variations.

Set up your meditation.

As you sit, think about the difference between these two mini practices:

- Doing three poses.

- Exploring three poses.

It's just numbers

*Hope lies in dreams,
in imagination and in the courage
of those who dare to make dreams into realities.*

JONAS SALK

If you've ever found yourself wishing, contemplating or dreaming about being a full-time yoga teacher, it's probably time to crunch some numbers. Before commencing on this black and white journey, keep in mind this exercise is to build perspective on possibilities and viabilities. Get out your paper or your spreadsheet and start gathering information.

Make a list of places where yoga classes are running in your location:

- How many of these classes are being taught each week?

- How many of these classes are you eligible to teach or interested in teaching?

- How many yoga classes are running privately?

- Think about one-on-one or in-home businesses.

On-line yoga grew exponentially during the COVID pandemic. Go on-line and look at sites and personalities that appeal to you or align with your personality or style of teaching:

- On-demand

- Live stream

If there are yoga classes in another form you are aware of, do your analysis.

Then, find out what the hourly or class or subscription or membership rates are for each of your locations.

When I did the math, I realized my yoga teaching style, age and preferences aligned with teaching at fitness clubs or private classes. I would need to teach three to five classes every day of the week to make a small income. This scenario was not good for me creatively, physically or financially.

I was working full time as an academic coach with the usual financial commitments to raising a family, paying a mortgage and all the other usual expenses.

My dream of teaching yoga would need to evolve from an interest to a livelihood, one step at a time.

Knowing what you want can be motivational, but understanding how to get there is essential.

Get out your paper or your tablets and create a series of *roadmaps* showing how you could travel from where you are today to where you want to be in the future:

If I teach yoga at (name the location), I would...

When all possibilities are explored, assess the energy output and the value input.

Wish, Dream, Plan

Write the first short phrases that come to mind when you think about your future self as a yoga teacher.

- Place these pieces of paper around your mat, word or image side up.

Assume your meditation seat.

Invite yourself into a practice where your eyes are closed, your breath is vibrant and your mind welcomes the concepts that come and go.

When your meditation is complete, revisit your phrases or record some new ideas.

As luck would have it

*Patience is the calm acceptance
that things can happen in a
different order than
the one you have in mind.*

DAVID G. ALLEN

There was a time when it appeared the yoga teaching space I was seeking might not appear.

I felt my volunteer teaching apprenticeship was complete. It was time to apply for a paying gig. My previous research narrowed my application plan to two fitness clubs: one, an exclusive multisport venue with an expensive membership price tag and the other, a smaller racquet and fitness club down the hill from my residence.

Interestingly, the club down the hill was the very same building where I first fell in love with yoga—although it had changed ownership several times and was renovated just as many. I was also a member, so I was familiar with the yoga studio, although I had not ever taken a class.

Both applications submitted.

No response.

More patience cultivated.

Sundays were a great day for me to grab a morning workout, but the trick was to arrive strategically before the yoga class started. For some reason, even though the teachers changed, the members loved this day and this time for their yoga—hence the parking challenge!

On one particular Sunday, I finished up my workout and decided to exit by the yoga studio—curious as to who was teaching and what the attendance was like. The studio was full, but there was no teacher.

No teacher and a full studio of eager yoga participants.

Was this my opportunity?

I gathered some courage, walked to the front desk and offered to teach the class. Me, the introverted future yoga teacher, offered to teach the class!

Motivated to keep the members content, I was ushered into the studio and introduced. Of course, I had my iPod with me, so I had access to all those yoga playlists I had been creating. With a quick intro to the sound system, I was left literally on the stage with a room full of humans on yoga mats; no plan, no sketchbook to teleprompt my yoga plan, no time to think about public speaking.

I couldn't believe I was in this situation. That I put myself in this situation.

I introduced myself, validating my status as a beginning teacher.

I couldn't tell you what I did that morning, but somehow I guided this group through a 45-minute yoga class complete with meditation, flow and Savasana.

After class, I stood at the door, wishing everyone a good day as they left the studio. I was showered with gratitude for a far from perfect, not even close to good, yoga class. But it was yoga and that was what they came for.

The group fitness manager sent me an email, thanking me for teaching the class; she gave me the information I would need to invoice the club for my time.

I had no intention of asking for payment—what I received on this day was more than I could have asked for. It filled me with such joy. Instead of making me more assertive to secure that yoga teaching position, it fortified my patience to wait for my time.

Think back to a time when you or your plan was stalled or rejected…

Where did it lead you?

How did you reset?

Simplify

Over time, I tried different sizes of notebooks and sketchbooks, all of which invited me to use yoga as a springboard to create...a masterpiece for the moment!

Sometimes I would invite myself to simplify the plan to increase both awareness and enjoyment.

Create a simple yoga class plan with layers of textures:

- Alternate words for...
- Season of the year...
- Peak or feature pose...
- An element of nature: sun, moon, sky...
- A significant word: love, balance, gratitude...
- Something else?

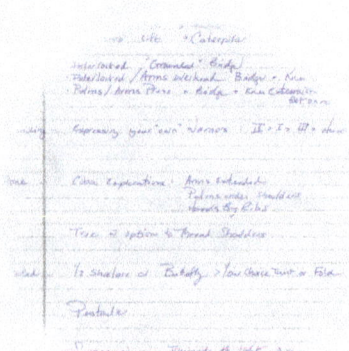

Image crisis

Sometimes people are beautiful.
Not in looks. Not in what they say.
Just in what they are.

MARKUS ZUSAK

It's funny the things we think about when we are commuting. Maybe more specifically, when traffic grinds to a halt with rush hour traffic. On one such occasion, I revisited my yoga teacher application plan. It had been a few months since my Sunday surprise class; I had noticed there seemed to be a few consistent teachers and a number of visiting teachers.

Maybe this would be the time to send another note to that fitness manager?

This logical, strategic thought was interrupted by a flurry of conflicting thoughts, all highlighting attire: what would I wear if I were to teach yoga as this club? When I stepped up to volunteer teach, I was wearing my usual workout attire: leggings, tank with built-in shelf bra and a long-sleeved top. Casual, athletic, comfortable.

But those yoga teachers I had been observing as I passed by the yoga studio were not wearing this ensemble. They were fit. Lots of skin showing, still athletic, but more than what I would be showing if I were in that position.

It was as if at that moment the lights went on and I became aware of the emerging *sexy* prototype of yoga teachers. Body beautiful is the universal theme of fitness, part of the visual landscape, but it was merely there, an entity separate from me. Now it was something I had to consider.

Yoga clothes need to support the body as it moves; no bulking layers to interfere with the asanas or the mat. My body, at this time, was the body of a woman in her fifties—no judgment here, just a fact: my skin and my body composition were very different than a woman in her twenties or thirties.

As luck would have it, there were a couple of longstanding yoga and fitness teachers at this club who were my age. They were uber-fit and beautiful to look at; their personalities, professionalism and their experience were enjoyed and respected.

This would take some reworking.

I needed to look the part, but on my terms. It seemed such a trivial issue, but this introvert required layers of preparation and attire for comfort and for self-confidence.

I once read that your home reflects who you are…

I wonder if this applies to our outer appearance?

What we present to the world, what others see, is like an introduction to who we are.

This is an interesting concept.

Yoga teachers don't wear a lot as the purpose of the practice is to deepen our connection to our bodies.

Take some time to consider this, no judging, no comparing, just looking at yoga teachers, their outward appearance and how it connects with who you think they are.

How does what you wear reflect who you are?

Living with fear stops us from taking risks. If you don't go out on the branch, you're never going to get the best fruit.

SARAH PARISH

Location

As time goes on, you will build fluency with yoga postures and transitions.

If you are keeping these plans, you may notice your tendency to flow and transition in a repeating pattern.

Try thinking about your planning from mat locations...

Design a yoga plan using the following outline as a guide:

- Seated
- Right Side, Left Side
- Prone
- Standing
- All Fours
- Supine

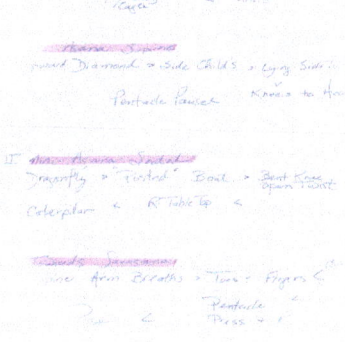

Creativity & Craft

Reading is a conversation.
All books talk.
But a good book listens as well.

MARK HADDON

Failing forward

*Courage allows the successful woman
to fail and learn powerful lessons from the failure.
So that in the end, she didn't fail at all.*

MAYA ANGELOU

December is an interesting month—so festive, but also reflective given the proximity of one year ending and another beginning.

As 2011 drew to a close, I was more ready than ever to officially begin my yoga teacher journey. Not as a volunteer. Not waiting for my opportunity to appear. Instead, I wanted to confidently step towards and land a regular, paid yoga teaching assignment.

So, I boldly emailed the group exercise manager from my fitness club, you remember, the one who personally thanked me for covering that Sunday class? Professionally and briefly, I asked whether there might be any yoga teacher openings in the new year.

My query was timely; there was an opening for a Thursday, 6pm yoga class at a sister facility. If I was interested, she would connect me with the club manager to set up an interview. Without sounding too eager, I accepted the opportunity.

The club manager was most gracious, seeing something in me that would work for this class. I sealed the deal by agreeing to teach a weekly Thursday 60-minute class; $24 per class would be my starting wage—if the numbers in my classes increased, so would my wage.

I was thrilled.

My preparation began three weeks prior to this debut. It was sketched, sequenced and scripted, complete with a supporting playlist.

On the first day of this class, I was ready from a yoga perspective, but my introverted self was a mess. If you share my affliction, fear of speaking in public, you can well imagine how my body was processing the stress of being center stage: nauseous seemed to be the simplest word to describe every layer of my being as I wrestled with the urge to take flight.

Although this was not the club I was familiar with, it was easy to check in, find the change rooms and locate the fitness studio. The class before me was a lively Zumba class…packed wall to wall.

It was January!

A glorious time for the fitness industry as it aligns revenue with new year's resolutions to get fit.

Then, it dawned on me, my first paid yoga class might also be packed!

Truthfully, it wouldn't matter how many attended my class, one or one hundred! I was a nervous mess.

With the change from Zumba to yoga underway, I became aware of something else. The teacher I was replacing was a bit of a hit. I learned she had moved on to pursue a teaching practice of her own, and it was clear, the number of participants entering the studio were not expecting this change.

I think my introduction and my obvious nervousness created a sense of empathy—no one left until my class was finished. My first class of over thirty-five participants was not exemplary, but I didn't think it would be. What I did was demonstrate my yoga teaching style, albeit at the beginning of my yoga teaching career. I had seven days to see how this announcement settled with the thirty or so yoga participants in this class.

The next Thursday, there were six participants—only two from the previous week. The other four were new members the club trainers encouraged to join a yoga class.

I was less nervous, but still nauseous. This smaller class, although not what the club would want, was a perfect second class for me. I was over-prepared, but stayed true to the vision of what my teaching style would be if I retained this gig long enough to get there!

Technically, if you compare the numbers between my first and my second class, I had failed—yet my self-confidence was in place: my path to finding my space as a yoga teacher would be long. I was patient and persistent enough to stay the course…whatever direction it took.

How does your body respond to stressful situations?

For me, it's an upset stomach and an extremely dry mouth.

How do you manage this discomfort to ease into what you find stressful?

For me, I've found I need to create space at the beginning where I don't speak very much—as I settle, the nausea fades and my dry mouth recalibrates.

To know yourself is to support yourself in these transitions...

I suspect even the most extroverted personality experiences stress and thus learns to manage it.

Stay open to the positive influences of transitional stress.

Asana Themes

Yoga asanas provide almost infinite possibilities for a practice, which is easy if you select your favorite postures.

But what if you selected a posture that is more of a challenge than a celebration?

The background for this planning invitation illustrates my decision to design a class around my least favorite collection of poses: backbends.

Go ahead.

Select a challenging pose and design an entire practice around this pose.

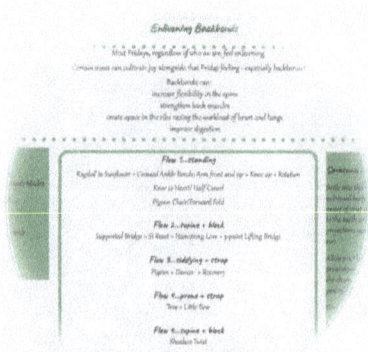

Reluctant learners wanted

Don't resist the change.
Be open to new possibilities.

AUTHOR UNKNOWN

It's true, I found great joy in teaching, first as a public educator, later as a yoga teacher, but I, myself, had never enjoyed learning until I was midway through my undergraduate degree in education.

Being a late bloomer, at least in understanding the joy of learning, has made for a series of interesting decisions: career-wise and life-wise. I had first-hand experience knowing what it feels like to wrestle with the discomfort of learning.

As others learned of my additional work as a teacher, now in the yoga classroom, I found myself having numerous yoga conversations—conversations that illuminated what many thought about yoga…and why they avoided trying it!

Yoga was coming on strong in professional sports, fitness facilities and classrooms. While some of these conversations seemed to focus on whether or not yoga was a religion, the most notable comments in my conversations were related to an individual's lack of flexibility as a reason to not do yoga.

The more I listened, the more I heard this correlation.

The more the correlation repeated itself, the more I realized the potential for my teaching niche…and it aligned beautifully with my yoga personal preference.

Those individuals who steered clear of yoga due to inflexibility were highly unlikely to head to the local yoga studio to be reminded just how inflexible they really were!

It also dawned on me that, while I demonstrated a joy for yoga, I did not present myself as highly flexible. Coming to yoga, even though that would change over time, my personal and my teaching practice had the potential to attract the most reluctant participant, because yoga isn't about starting out as flexible, it's about creating a strong connection between mind, body and breath.

I also accepted that I would not attract the super flexible yogis—my style of teaching would not engage or challenge them. There were a multitude of studios and teachers who could offer practices suited to the aspirations of the advanced yoga.

For me, the more reluctant yogi, the better!

As a child, I was more of a reluctant learner.

As an adult, this became my super power when I saw the potential to attract reluctant yogis to their mats because of my own experiences with reluctance and learning.

What is your super power?

How will this attract others to your classes?

STRENGTH & SURRENDER

To understand who you might attract to your yoga classes will shape the kind of practices you design.

If you are more on the athletic side, your practices may feature more advanced sequencing of asansas.

If you seek the quieter side of yoga, you may enjoy designing and teaching yin or restorative or gentle yoga.

I wanted to attract the reluctant yogis which meant my plans might be simpler in design to allow minds and bodies to open more to practicing yoga on a regular basis.

Take some time to plan a practice using the following leads:

- Who do you envision being attracted to your classes?

- How will you select and sequence a class for this type of yogi or yogini?

- When the design is finished, do the practice yourself or find a place to teach this class!

Say it don't show it

*Life is about perspective
and how you look at something...
ultimately, you have to zoom out.*

WHITNEY WOLFE HERD

My weekly Thursday yoga class numbers began to grow, from six participants to anywhere between ten to fifteen. These numbers were in line with other yoga classes at the sister club facilities.

I knew I had some time, maybe even a long time, to more fully explore my teaching style with some regulars now attending each week.

The nervousness before teaching had leveled off; no more nausea, but still the dry mouth persisted at the start of class. I could say I was getting comfortable with teaching yoga, which is not what I was striving for—being comfortable is a neon sign indicating it's time to make a change.

My planning and preparation before each class remained creative; I maintained my goal to not teach the same class twice. I was gaining confidence by doing the practice I taught on a small stage at the center of the studio, as well as speaking the words for auditory guidance throughout the practice. In fact, this is what was being done in most fitness studios, and it worked because the visual component enabled all participants to see what they should be doing on their mats.

Most yoga teacher trainings emphasize the development of cuing the practice with words and maybe a bit of demonstration. I was doing too much of the class.

I remember when I had enough yoga experience to look less and feel more.

I remember how liberating it was to prioritize the auditory focus and release the visual dependency.

I wanted to become that yoga teacher who could, with time and practice, cue a class without doing the practice.

This was a risky move as it could potentially create discomfort for the members who were so accustomed to watching the yoga teacher as they practiced yoga. How could I begin this transitional change in teaching style in a thoughtful and progressive manner?

I made the decision to pick one section each week to *say not show*.

The safest time in the practice to try this was Savasana. I could start the guided relaxation from the stage, then walk around the room so they would hear and feel my presence from different locations in the room. Their eyes would be closed; there were no complicated sequences. When I brought them out of Savasana, I was back at my teaching space in front of the class.

Next, it was the opening meditation.

Then gradually, speaking the sequences within a section or two of the class. This became so intriguing for me and my classes, especially when I would surprise them by creating different stages in the room. Those who liked to be at the back of the studio would sometimes find themselves at the front of the class as I changed my teaching position.

Planning is a platform for generating practice plans but every so often I found myself in what I would call a cuing slump.

If I sounded redundant to myself, imagine how redundant I must sound to my class participants!

When this happens, I like to inspire my planning with, "What if?"

I wondered, on several occasions, if I could lead a class without doing or naming the postures...I'd often tell the class in advance so they could become part of the experience.

Try teaching a class without saying the names, English or Sanskrit, or doing any of any of the postures you are teaching—words only.

What did you discover...

Novel

To make a change from doing the class with the students, think about your class design from a new perspective.

One example might be to take a flow like Moon Salutations.

The flow begins facing the long edge of the mat and transitions to one short edge, the other short edge and then back to facing the long edge.

If this is already familiar to you, think about something else to turn the familiar into refreshing.

Some examples:

- Plan a class without standing postures.
- Integrate short meditations throughout the practice.
- Begin with a focused Savasana and end with a moving meditation.

Think the design differently and the cues will become the guide.

Design it.

Then find a space to *cue* it!

Foreigner in a familiar land

*My happiness grows in
direct proportion to my acceptance,
and in inverse proportion
to my expectations.*

MICHAEL J. FOX

We have all had the experience—usually when we're alone—of hearing a conversation in a language other than our own. If this experience happens in a closed space over a long period of time, we notice the changes in volume, tone and intonation. We can guess whether the conversation is serious, humorous, professional or friendly. And eventually, we tune out the conversation, because we don't understand the nuances.

The first time I heard Sanskrit being spoken was in a yoga class at a local yoga studio. I loved hearing the intonations of this mystifying language, but found myself annoyingly a step or two behind the sequence.

Others in the class, clearly more fluent than I, were completely in sync with the teacher's language. I became more aware of my lack of understanding as it compared to the seemingly effortless comprehension of the majority of the other participants.

Fluency in the Sanskrit language appears to enhance the practice for many. But not for me. Those fluent in Sanskrit, particularly yoga teachers, can unknowingly or intentionally create a divide.

I recall sharing a teaching space with two retired yoga teachers. When I referenced a yoga pose called Warrior Two, the elder of the two asked what I meant and the other clarified, "She means Virabhadrasana II."

Perhaps it was a moment of clarification between the two, but it felt a bit like yoga snobbery.

This only deepened my resolve to be a strong communicator in the yoga classroom so as to ensure all participants could first understand the movement before customizing their experience on their mats.

> **What is your relationship with Sanskrit?**
>
> How does this relationship shape the language you will develop as a yoga teacher?

Leading Words

If I find my idea bank low on energy, I often switch my mindset from yoga to words.

Over the years, I have been astonished how a single word infuses my design with renewed energy.

In one instance, I focused on the word *joy* which lead to a series of inquiries:

- How does joy feel?
- When do I feel joy in my yoga practice?
- What does joy look like when participants in my class experience it?

This lead me to a quote, "Joy is portable, bring it with you!"

Moving to your mat, see what words come to mind.

Follow your teaching instincts:

- Select a word or phrase.
- Let the words lead the design.

The language of yoga

Less is the new more.

UNKNOWN

As is the case with most 200-hour yoga teacher trainings, there is a curricular segment on Sanskrit, the language of yoga. This section of my YTT curriculum came hot on the heels of the anatomy section. Maybe one of the most significant epiphanies of my training was the realization of how much I didn't know about the human body. Sure, I was fluent in general terms, but not anatomically.

My mind was reeling with this gap: how could I have lived so long in this body and know so little about it?

Then we began the Sanskrit section. It was both beautiful and mystical to listen to. The course instructors were fluent in Sanskrit, but I found myself lost in translation when I was practicing, due to my increased desire to become more aware of anatomy and yoga.

As a learner and a future yoga teacher, I didn't see myself investing the time to learn Sanskrit.

I had a different language priority: to speak the language of human anatomy.

While I was building anatomical fluency, I practiced cuing poses and transitions in English rather than Sanskrit. My goal was to explore ways to increase the connection between body and brain while enriching anatomical awareness for those in my practice.

The purpose of language is, among many other things, to communicate and to connect.

This awareness intensifies your gift as a teacher: your voice is your connection to your participants.

What language do you respond to when you practice?

What language will you utilize when you teach?

How will the language you speak *communicate and connect*?

Body Language

I aim to *learn* every time I have the opportunity to *design and teach* a yoga class.

To become more fluent with human anatomy, I would often connect the dots.

For example, if I planned to teach Child's Pose, I'd explore the anatomical parts most influenced by the pose:

- In prone Child's Pose, I might bring awarness to the spine.

- In supine Child's Pose, I might bring awareness to the hips.

- In other variations, I might flow between Puppy and Child's Pose with spine, hip and shoulder awareness.

Think about your yoga teaching language and plan a yoga class with more connected dots!

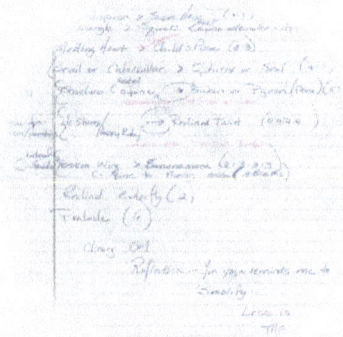

Springboard to design

What we see is often only a fractional part of what it really is.

AUTHOR UNKNOWN

Curiosity pairs beautifully with learning; it invites exploration without the expectation of knowing all the right answers. My peaked interest in anatomy put me on a quest to learn more, not as deeply as a medical professional, but as broadly as could potentially apply to teaching yoga.

Over time, I collected several beautiful, technical and helpful anatomy resources for my physical library. I also tried some of the anatomy apps, but truly found my best learning happened when I studied physical books. The books providing the most clarity often had illustrations, artfully created, of the human body in motion.

The integration of anatomical details into my practice followed the pattern of my studies: learn a little, teach a little. As I was learning, so were the participants in my classes.

Sometimes I would weave anatomy throughout a flow; other times I would build a practice around a specific anatomical location.

Eventually, the fluency with what I call my working anatomy knowledge became my style of teaching. Instead weaving Sanskrit into my cuing, I wove anatomical terms, both general and scientific.

> **The learning springboard is a key element integral your development as a unique yoga teacher.**
>
> Over time, it will define a style that is your own.
>
> **If you want to build a business around teaching yoga, you will need to be familiar but unique.**
>
> What are the springboards of interest that could expand your teaching style and define a possible niche market?

Digging Deeper

It's easy to find many practices dedicated to opening hips.

Which is a good thing given most humans benefit from hip work.

What if you took this popular yoga class focus and added depth to your design?

Hip Opening Poses	Range of Motion	Anatomy: Above and Below

You are welcome to pick a different focus and complete the chart using the three frames.

Once charted, design your class.

If you have an opportunity, teach this class and pay attention to how digging deeper shapes your delivery.

Hands on, hands off

Our bodies are our gardens—
our wills are our gardeners.

WILLIAM SHAKESPEARE

There have been so many shifts on so many levels of life, locally and globally, especially with regard to the temple that is the human body: when to touch, when to compliment, when to acknowledge, how to address, how to greet and more.

When I took my teacher training, there was a strong emphasis on alignment and the value of hands-on adjustments. I'll admit, I have benefitted greatly by having expert hands on my body making slight adjustments to take me into a pose with new awareness. But I struggled with putting my hands on others, especially when I had so little yoga experience and was newly acquainted with human anatomy.

I was a hands-off yoga teacher in large class settings, but I wondered how I could help others feel what I had felt with words only. The better my cues became and the more I wove anatomy into the class, it seemed as if the geography of the body had more clarity—for some.

There were others, no matter how many times I cued them or practiced beside them or spoke specifically to them, they demonstrated little or no body awareness. The disconnect between the brain and the body was mystifying to me as a teacher.

It occurred to me one Sunday that I could invite those interested in a deeper discussion of downward facing dog to stay after class. Five interested women accepted my invitation and we discussed ways to improve this pose from an alignment and anatomical perspective. It was also at this time, I learned more medical history so when I did an adjustment, I had consent, information and a public space to do so.

Would these eager yogis have wanted more adjustments? Absolutely, but this was not to be a strong element of my group yoga teaching; instead, it became a future practice design called: *Hands on Me*.

> **When you think about your experiences with *#metoo* or *woke* culture, what are some of your *awakenings* to life?**
>
> How might these influence your teaching practice and your relationships with your students?

Your Hands, Your Yoga

To increase body awareness in a yoga class, try some of these cue combos:

- Breath work with your hands on your front ribs, then your side ribs to feel how breath moves in a meditation.
- Place your hands on your pelvis for Warrior I then Warrior II to feel the position of the hips and spine in each of these postures.
- Align the outside of your lead Warrior I foot, the foot bones between the fifth toe and the outer ankle bone, on the long edge of your yoga mat, to feel a parallel foot position.

Each of these cues connects awareness of anatomy to yoga which could, ultimately, increase the connection between body and brain.

Design a simple practice of 4-6 asanas.

With each pose, create a few cues for your own *hands on me* class design!

You can't change that

Innovation is the ability to see change as an opportunity—not a threat.

STEVE JOBS

Yoga is steeped in traditions, it has been since its inception.

Depending on where you study or how you practice, you may have an affinity or a preference for a specific style of yoga. Sometimes, affinities and preferences are coupled with strong opinions that create boundaries around what is acceptable and what is not.

If yoga traditions didn't evolve:

- Yoga would not be practiced on a mat; mats were invented in 1982. Before that, yogis practiced on whatever surface was available.

- Women would not be fully represented in yoga classes; more women began to participate and teach yoga in the early 1970's.

- Yoga would only be taught in Northern India, yoga's birthplace.

- We would not be having conversations about finding your place as a yoga teacher today!

This is a different time.

Thankfully.

Yoga has changed from the fringe to the main stage, from those into new age to anyone interested in learning how to move with greater ease. As it continues to evolve and be accessible, there are so many types of yoga, it's hard to believe there isn't a yoga style for everyone!

The timing of my entrance to teaching yoga was on this new wave of yoga. Right when I was gaining traction with the belief I would attract participants who wanted to experience change on their mat, yoga was changing dramatically.

Naked yoga. Goat yoga. Laughing yoga. Swearing yoga. Yoga for Christians. Yoga for pregnant women. Yoga for large women. Yoga for PTSD. Yoga for depression. Yoga for arthritis. Yoga was for anything, anywhere, everything and everybody!

The more diverse the yoga options, the more challenging it might be for me to build my business. More than ever, I stayed true to my belief: there would be space for me to teach.

I maintained my teaching goal to design new practices every week. Doing so was defining my participants. Those wanting a familiar Ashtanga or Hatha or Bikram class sequence would find themselves frustrated or out of sync with the other participants in my classes. Some would stay, sometimes just practicing on their own or they would, with obvious frustration, follow my cues or they would simply roll up their mat and leave.

Those that left, I never saw again.

As challenging having students walk out of your class is to a teacher's confidence, it's an important reminder that all adults have a choice—just as I had a choice to stay within the familiar yoga sequencing I was taught in my training or to wander in the creative zone.

The more I stayed with my style, the more I noticed what I already knew: adults, as they age, typically navigate towards comfort and familiarity.

Learning is awkward.

Coming onto a yoga mat without a clue as to what the yoga teacher will be doing reminds adults to be curious rather than critical.

It's a huge shift in mindset—more open, more receptive, less rigid, less judgmental. I often hoped my yoga practice would open my students' hearts and minds to other possibilities in their lives.

As a teacher, challenging myself to create new sequences for the participants who have practiced with me over the years, some of them ten years, gave me, in turn, the gifts of curiosity, novelty, innovation, creativity, challenge and comfort. Thus, I think I have become more receptive, youthful, creative and aware of my potentially limiting patterns.

In essence, the learner leading the class meets the learners on the mat and, most times, a kind of energetic magic occurs as we practice together...we both want to repeat this learning experience when we meet again on our mats.

Think back to a time when you were ready to learn something, but the instructor had different ideas.

> Where were you?
>
> What did you think you were going to learn?
>
> What did the instructor want to teach?
>
> How did you navigate this discrepancy?

Think about yourself as yoga teacher. There is no one way to teach, but there is a way you teach.

> Describe your way…

Remaining consistent can be as powerful as inviting change.

> What is the relationship between change and consistency in your life and in your teaching?

I would also add, when life deals those difficult cards (death, divorce, unemployment, injury, etc.), it is comforting to settle into a familiar practice on the mat.

> What are your *go to* familiar yoga comforts?

Gone Rogue

Yoga is rich in history, traditions and innovation.

It's important to respect the past but equally important to be a trailblazer.

When I merge yoga with strength training or yoga with mobility or yoga with an element of surprise, I create intriguing names:

- MoBY = Mobility Balance Yoga
- Rogue Yoga = Yoga off the grid
- Yoga Bells = Yoga with light dumbbells
- Sticks & Stones = Yoga with mobility balls and dowels

Not everyone will love this kind of class creation but, for me, it's exhilarating to think of all the possibilities.

Give it a try…merge something of interest with a yoga plan.

If the opportunity presents, share it!

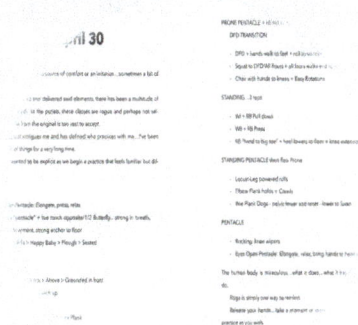

A space to teach

*Each day is a gift...
don't send it back unopened.*

AUTHOR UNKNOWN

Teaching is more than who teaches a class. Teaching is more than who takes a class. These roles, teacher-participant, merge in a space of time called the present.

Teaching is more than where you teach. More than walls, floors, lighting. More than curriculum, sequencing, sounds. Much, much more than yoga.

For a defined period of time, teacher and participants enter a shared space without fully realizing who we are, who we will become, who we were. When we look at teaching a class as entering a special or sacred time and space, we invite ourselves to prepare differently.

Thus, preparing to teach yoga is much more than a series of asanas, a yoga space and a period of time.

> If yoga is more than asansas, space and time, what is it to you?

A Gift

There have been so many occasions when I felt deep gratitude for the opportunities to teach.

This gratitude often makes its way into my practice designs.

On one occasion, I converted the concept of gratitude to the concept of gift.

The sequence of asanas was labeled:

- Supine Gifts
- Standing Gifts
- Core Gifts
- Floor Gifts
- Savasana Gifts

See if you can create a practice using the concept of gift and these headings.

- Is there another word or concept you could use to ignite alternate ways of thinking about class design?

Have you ever

*A mentor is someone who allows you
to see the hope inside yourself.*

OPRAH WINFREY

Have you ever found yourself in a live yoga class with an exceptional yoga specimen in a teaching role?

Usually, this human is a local yoga celebrity. The studio, however peaceful, vibrates with excitement. And when the teacher makes an appearance, regardless of what individuals are doing on their mats, there is a collective joyful response:

> In awe to simply be in the same yoga space with this celestial being.

Regardless of sex or gender, this specimen is aesthetically beautiful—perfectly proportioned with that right blend of athleticism and grace. Even before this human begins to speak, all you want to do is watch what they do on their mat.

Most often, you don't need to wait long. This is what they were born to do: yoga.

Yoga that looks like a ballet or gymnastics mat routine or an awe-inspiring Cirque de Soleil act...which is nothing like what you are doing on your mat!

The class continues, advancing through basic asansas, progressing perfectly to more advanced poses until the moment you've been waiting for arrives.

This incredible specimen, and maybe a few other able-bodied participants, is sequencing through arm balances, headstands and more advanced postures.

There is no hope that today, or ever, you will do these postures. Even entertaining the thought of trying sets you up for an injury. But to be there, watching from whatever substitute yoga pose you've crafted feels surreal. Although your practice is completely different from the one being taught, you feel as though you vicariously did the same advanced practice.

When you leave, you wonder, even though you already know, if you'll ever be like that yoga human. The thought somehow elevates your spirit and permeates your practices for the next few days.

And then you settle into your own routine.

There are always going to be super yogis, super athletes and super human beings. The rest of us can't compete for these spaces, but we can be inspired to create similarly inspiring spaces; just you and your teaching gifts.

Who is your version of a yoga celebrity?

What are this celebrity's gifts?

It's possible some future participant might see your extraordinary gifts.

What are those gifts that you possess?

Inspired By

Excellent teaching inspires others to teach with excellence.

While exploring your own teaching style, take some time to be taught and experience excellence as a student of yoga.

- Take a class from your local favorite celebrity teacher.

After the class, find a space to soak up the brilliance of the class and recreate the practice… as best you can remember.

Then, when the time is right, revise this practice to align with your own teaching style and teach it to someone else.

Injury is an excellent teacher

*Sometimes stillness is
the best movement.*

JCLAY

In the early years of my yoga teaching, the only way I found the courage to teach was to practice a zillion times before leading a class. I was feeling great—teaching one class per week, but in reality was I was teaching many more classes with me, myself and I.

And then it started. Just that nagging sensation in my left shoulder. Yoga is good for the body, right?

So, I kept doing my preparation routine; the nagging sensation changed to something much more uncomfortable. Then something painful, to the point I was changing how I moved to minimize the discomfort: putting on a coat, taking something out of the fridge, putting on my seatbelt. As the pain increased, I also strategically took Advil to ensure my teaching was not disrupted.

I was in that space where everything I was doing was making my injury worse. Finally, I initiated the process to better understand the injury and restore my shoulder's health: physiotherapists, chiropractors, acupuncturists, hydrotherapy, body rolling and more.

The diagnosis was frozen shoulder; not an uncommon issue for menopausal or post-menopausal women. I was faced with the decision to accept and move into cortisone therapy or truly look at my practice and movement patterns.

There was no doubt, the essence of my injury stemmed from using the vinyasa as a transition. While I had creatively strayed from using it every transition, I was clearly using it too much.

If I was to continue teaching yoga, I needed to heal.

If I was to heal, I needed to change how I utilized transitions in the practice.

I went back to my anatomy books to learn more about the shoulder.

I stopped doing vinyasas, downward facing dogs and upward facing dogs in my personal and my teaching practice. I changed how I put on my jacket. I started using my left and right arms in a more balanced way throughout the day. And I found a gifted therapist who used IMS (intramuscular stimulation) to release the pattern of injury from my body.

When I was finally free from pain, I committed to protecting others from the same misery. I started to rethink and create movement patterns, which in turn, changed my practices completely: planks, down dogs and vinyasas were eliminated from my teaching practice.

At first, I didn't notice any difference with the class participants—I changed things up every week so this seemed like another change.

But then I did notice something was different.

Three of my most dedicated students, all quite fit and focused, were no longer my regulars.

What are the patterns of pain, discomfort or injury in your body?

> How do you heal?

> Who are your healers?

> What have your injuries taught you?

Who are your mentors or those who inspire you?

> What is their pattern of injury?

Even the most amazing bodies in fitness and yoga are vulnerable to injury; most are willing to share their healing stories.

> I recall Yamuna, Jill Miller, Kathryn Budig…and all otherworldly teachers, all honest about their issues, surgeries and recoveries.

In Stillness

It's easy to stay focused on class designs and preparation for others.

It's important to preserve time and space to restore and rejuvenate yourself along your teaching journey.

Take a short detour and learn the essentials of a restorative yoga practice.

Do the same for a yin yoga practice.

Find a sequence or register for one or both of these classes.

Then design a simple restorative or yin practice for yourself to do every four weeks.

Kindly criticized

*Learning and knowing
I can explain it to you,
but I can't understand it for you.*

AUTHOR UNKNOWN

One of my regular Sunday yogis asked me to meet her for coffee. We caught up on life and then she hinted she needed discuss something with me. She volunteered to share some feedback: a few people from my Sunday yoga class had been discussing the changes in my teaching. They felt my sequencing wasn't challenging enough anymore.

I was not prepared for this. My natural response was to feel a bit defensive, but at the same time, I was curious to learn more.

It was pretty simple: down dogs and vinyasas were synonymous with having a good workout. I wasn't providing them, thus the optics of my Sunday yoga class was that the class had become too easy.

I knew, teaching in a fitness facility, that yoga was considered part of a fitness routine. I considered it to be an element of my own fitness.

I had been challenged as a teacher to plan transitions differently due to my injury and my concern for others being injured, but some of the participants were no longer feeling challenged when they practiced.

Not doing a dozen or more vinyasas resulted in less exertion, and thus equated with not having a good workout.

Truthfully, I didn't leave this coffee date feeling great.

Of course, my ego was bruised as I, and only I, knew just how much effort went into the smallest details of every class I designed.

But this was a most generous gift: an opportunity to rethink and expand my preparation. After all, I had, to a small degree, started to add gentle planks and modified downward facing dogs back into my personal practice.

There is always an awkwardness when truths are shared; how they are managed paves the way for building long and bountiful relationships with others. This beautiful woman remained one of my regulars for quite some time after this conversation, and I'm still delighted when I meet her on a neighborhood walking path.

I was inspired to find ways to increase my fluency with modifications. This was part of the teacher training, but there were so many other layers I needed to attend to, it wasn't until this time and this conversation that I had the maturity, experience and insight to advance my teaching.

How do you handle the proverbial *sh*t sandwich*?

Some suggestions have value, others simply need to be acknowledged.

What is your process for sifting and sorting to find the value?

Finding Peace

You will spend hours reflecting, preparing, planning and self-assessing.

You will feel yourself progressing and evolving as a teacher.

But every so often, you will deal with, what feels like, criticism.

It can cause stress.

> *And self-doubt.*

It can challenge confidence.

> *And cast a shadow.*

There are many ways to reset, one of them is to focus on inner peace.

Bring yourself to your mat.

Think about peace, being peaceful, feeling at peace...then let your asanas present themselves.

When you are finished, document this peaceful practice and keep it in an easy to access space for the future.

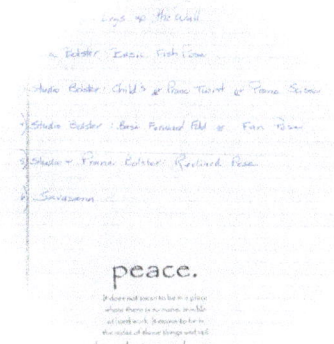

Inclusively exclusive

Peace does not need to be in a place.

AUTHOR UNKNOWN

Good advice can surface from challenging conversations—so long as the defense mechanisms are turned off and the intention originates from an honest space.

As I digested the feedback from my Sunday coffee conversation, I realized my goal to be different from the Olympic-level yogis created an unexpected issue: I was designing for the inexperienced or reluctant yogi and had, in turn, ignored the interests of the more athletic or experienced yogi.

There is always room for improvement. I needed to improve my verbal cues to be more inclusive for both the new and the seasoned participant. I also wondered what other areas of my teaching practice needed refinement.

The answer would not accurately surface from my memory; it would present itself if I went back through my teaching plans.

My practice archive!

I was still using sketchbooks. Every practice was dated, making it easy to review my notes. This analysis evidenced a good variety of themes, music and inspirations, but I could see I seemed to be avoiding breath work and spirit work.

The location for most of my classes was still at the fitness club, so spirit work would need to remain as it was, but the breath work had potential. My challenge would be the pacing—I only had sixty minutes and already I struggled with finishing on time. The goal was to weave breath work into what I was already doing, rather than making it an add-on.

Gradually, breath awareness cues were added to the flow, then to the Savasana, and finally to the opening meditation. Adding small amounts of breath work seamlessly wove into an ever-changing practice plan. I relearned the elements of breath work, some from my training, some from my ongoing studies, and shared this learning week by week.

I still find value reviewing my practice plans.

It's easy to fall into patterns, but I remain committed to evolving as a learner first, and then as a learner who teaches what she has learned.

How are you keeping track of your yoga journey: your past and your present and maybe even notes for the future?

Time for an audit...

What are your patterns of repetition?

Where are your patterns of innovation?

How are you evolving as a yoga teacher?

I Quote You

Words written by others, famous or unknown, have been a continuous source of inspiration... especially if my energy is low.

If I am inspired by quotes, it kindles my creative spirit and my yoga plans emerge, recharged by the words of someone else.

Find a new quote, one you haven't heard before but immediately resonates with you.

Write it down.

Close your eyes and allow the words to permeate your meditation.

When you are ready, open your eyes and see what class design presents itself.

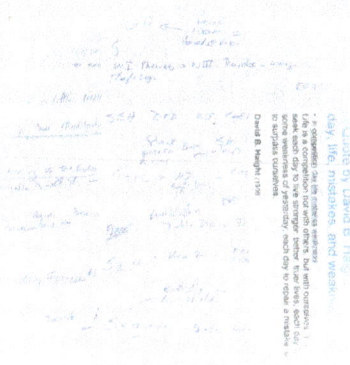

Guess who's coming to practice

*The pose you avoid the most,
you need the most.*

AUTHOR UNKNOWN

Where you teach will shape how you teach. In my case, I could have as few as six participants or as many as seventy on any given Sunday that yoga was offered at the fitness club.

On any of these days, I might recognize some participants, but there was always someone new. The participants ranged from teens to seniors; male and female; fit and not fit; in a good mood or in a somber mood. There were classes where I connected with the group; there were classes where I didn't.

There seemed always to be a class where someone left early—sometimes close to the beginning, but mostly as we were setting up for Savasana. It became a fascination of mine to see if I could teach a class where no one left early. Or, to teach a class where that individual who didn't want to be there was pleased they came.

As I considered all these variables, I focused on finding as many layers to engage the participants as possible.

And then I realized I was learning about the business of yoga.

It might sound silly, but truthfully my teaching focus was diminishing my fear of public speaking. I was now on a journey to teach in a classroom where every student chooses to be there.

The more I thought about the business of yoga, the more I thought about other places where my teaching and my business might merge.

The game of guessing who would come to class shifted to who would come to my class if I taught somewhere else?

Just as I was musing, one of the regular participants asked if I taught anywhere else and if I would consider teaching a private yoga class for some women in her small business. My answer then, as it is now, was, "Let's give it a try."

> **There will come a time, if it hasn't come already, when you will sense a participant's disapproval of you, your teaching or simply your class.**
>
> **It may be expressed via body language, facial expressions or simply leaving your class before the end.**
>
> How will you acknowledge disapproval and then let it go?

Practicing Disapproval

To get comfortable with inevitable disapproval, I routinely design a practice with a yoga asanas I disapprove of...no matter how often I practice or how many different variations I create, I disapprove of the pose.

The pose is pigeon pose.

To shift my thinking, I move to my mat and wonder how I could create pigeon pose from:

- Seated position
- Standing position
- Supine position
- Prone position
- Side lying position
- With a prop

Maybe you have a different pose that you disapprove of.

Try designing a practice using mat locations for your disapproval pose.

Copy then create

*Imitation is the sincerest form of flattery...
so don't be cross, it's a compliment!*

AUTHOR UNKNOWN

There were patches when I wondered if I could create another new practice—realistically, how many ways can yoga asanas be programmed? When I entered this zone, it was time to browse sources other than my experience and imagination.

One of my constant sources of inspiration was *The Yoga Journal*, so much so, I subscribed to the magazine for several years. I loved the aesthetic of yoga, but the magazine also had tremendous teaching elements I could extract and rework for my practice designs.

The sequences that were published could never be used as published due, perhaps, to the use of props. There were no yoga props at the fitness club or at the space where I was teaching privately and very often, the asanas progressed towards more challenging variations that would be difficult to utilize given the participants' wide range of yoga levels varying from week to week.

I selected a sequence I liked, brought it to my sketchbook and explored ways to weave the featured magazine elements into my practice design.

Sometimes, the sequence inspired the creation of something new; other times, it simply inspired what I was already doing. All was well until one woman casually mentioned that her other yoga teacher was also doing a heart opening sequence. Heart opening sequences were the theme of the latest edition of *The Yoga Journal* and the foundation for my practice that day.

Of course, it was possible other yoga teachers would be doing what I was doing!

I altered my approach: I stopped utilizing the current issue; instead, I mined the magazine archives for inspiration.

Like most things, *The Yoga Journal* eventually stopped being an ongoing source of inspiration, although it occasionally still catches my eye.

So, I moved on…to the yoga section of the book store!

> **Where do you source inspiration for your teaching designs?**
>
> How do you go beyond the surface to understand, to rework and customize designs for your teaching practice or your participants?

Your Re-creation

By now, you have likely connected to a yoga social channel or a publication.

This connection yields layers of inspiration for your personal and your teaching practice.

However, you will need to reshape the content to ensure it aligns with you and your participants.

Find one practice that inspires you:

- Review the sequencing.

- Follow the sequence for your personal practice.

- Observe the moments where the flow is interrupted.

- Now think about the practice, using those interruptions as space for you to inject your style of teaching.

- Reorganize, add your voice and design a practice you could teach...giving credit, of course, to the source of your re-creation!

What's on your shelf

Reading is dreaming with open eyes.
UNKNOWN

True confession. I admit, I adore books...in book stores, in my hands, on my bookshelves.

I also admit, I'm a recovering book addict—my shelves used to be loaded beyond capacity. There were books I had never read, books I had partially read and books I had read several times. Just when there was little or no shelf real estate, I crossed paths with a little book called *Spark Joy*.

Following the expert guidance of Marie Kondo, the shelves were put to the Kondo test: categorized by subject or author, read or not read, keep or donate...even those books that were in the yoga category.

By this time, I had an assortment of yoga books, from my teacher trainings to the latest publications. Some were theoretical, others practical and still others autobiographical. I needed a selection process; if I wasn't going to put these yoga books to good use, I knew someone would.

The essential culling question was: will this yoga book spark creative joy for future yoga practices, for myself or for those I teach?

While I remain open to adding to my library, all future purchases must pass this same essential question: will it inspire me to create new yoga practices?

There are some books that have a special place on my shelves. They speak to me consistently and, amazingly, despite all the times I've looked at them, they still inspire me. The most frequently sourced books for my creations are those written by Sage Rountree: her practice designs are accessible and adjustable for anyone; her philosophy is applicable for everyone; her wisdom is insightful for those who teach.

The process I use when I'm sourcing books for class design inspiration is the same as what I did with *The Yoga Journal*:

- Find a nugget.

- Reflect on its potential.

- Then weave it into the creative process.

This allows my teaching voice to flourish as I design, which in turn, will inspire my participants.

I often name Sage when I introduce the class. I've encouraged others to purchase her books.

I make it clear who inspires my teaching or what inspires my teaching. I do so to plant seeds for them to be inspired to seek and weave yoga elements into their lives.

Are you a reader?

Not everyone is.

That's okay because…there are audio books!

If your budget doesn't allow for the purchase of books, the public library provides access to a wide assortment of books, all you need is a library card.

Accessing the power of books will maintain your status as a learner, which is essential if you want to be an evolving teacher.

What books have inspired you?

What's on your want to read list?

Who is your Sage Rountree?

Most Worn Pages

The most well worn pages on my bookshelves are books by Sage Rountree, in particular, her beautiful framework for the spine.

I have created numerous practices using her six moves of the spine, citing her as the expert but crafting language and sequencing specific for those registered for the class.

As always, I create from my mat...six moves of the spine from:

- Supine
- Prone
- All Fours
- Seated
- Standing

Create a practice using an inspirational framework from the most worn pages of your library.

When I grow up

*Be fearless in the pursuit
of what sets your soul on fire.*

UNKNOWN

As you already know, Sage Rountree's teaching is one foundation of my teaching. But before her, I was completely in awe of Shiva Rea. I came across Rea's style of teaching when I was looking for visual inspiration back in the day before streaming, a time when videos could be purchased and downloaded from iTunes.

First, I was drawn to where she taught: Greece. I was seduced by the warmth emanating from the background, the sky and the sea. Second, it was her flowing movements, infused by the lyrical cues to transition, to be, to feel.

Even though there were segments of her flow beyond my abilities and those I taught, there was something accessible—a primal invitation to try and then discover some vibration within.

While I was working on my yoga creations, I practiced with Shiva. I used the Internet to research the locations for her classes and her teacher training, but her offerings were outside of my reach financially and practically.

Then, as if the yoga goddesses were listening, I learned Shiva Rea had written a book. I marked down the release date and pre-ordered her book. I wondered, if I read her words, could I integrate more of her style into my own.

The book, *Tending to the Heart's Fire*, arrived and met all of my expectations, but I didn't feel it provided me with insights that were transferable to my teaching practice.

So, I did what I had been doing. I looked for a nugget, that element I could extract and weave into an authentic practice. The sequence would be perfect for a private class I was now teaching—this was a class without beginners, plus it had a few advanced yoginis.

I selected music by Stevin McNamara, similar to the Rea's videos: primal beat, pulsing strings, quietly energizing. I practiced the movements and the cues prior to the class.

To capture the attention of the participants, I started the class by saying, "This class is inspired by a woman I want to be when I grow up."

I received laughter of course—I was in my mid-fifties!

The response after class was enthusiastic. Sure it was the novelty of Shiva's style, but mostly it was the connection we make when we teach, sharing elements of our common experience as human beings.

Everyone in that class had, at one time of another, a Shiva Rea-spiration.

We all need these inspirations.

They are supplements for our soul, especially when we invite the inspiration, but make it our own while giving credit where credit is due.

There is no doubt celebrity worship can be inspirational and yoga has its fair share of celebrities.

Such influences need to be measured.

> It's too easy to find yourself in the audience, watching, reading, or being entertained.

I'm on a different wavelength, almost looking upon sources of inspiration with a high filter.

> My time is precious, so precious, I hope I have enough time in my life to do what I want to do. I have no time to waste watching.

When you are sourcing your inspiration, I encourage you to do the same thing.

> That said, is there a yoga personality or philosophy that resonates with you?

> How does it shape your life or your practice or something else?

How much is enough

Education isn't something you can finish.

UNKNOWN

When I first completed my 200-hour yoga teacher training, it was recognized as a qualifier to teach in any facility. I also had an undergraduate and graduate degree in education, so I easily qualified for my current and future positions.

But I wanted to learn more.

I wanted to learn more about yoga, fitness, anatomy and psychology. Just as I had done with my yoga training, I researched my options and determined it would be beneficial to acquire a certification to teach group fitness. I selected a provincial certification program, took the courses, passed the exam and acquired the liability insurance.

When this training was complete, I also wondered about certifying to become a personal trainer. It seemed possible at this early phase of my wellness career that one-on-one sessions could be a viable revenue stream for the future. This time, I selected a national group to certify with, canfitpro, took the courses, completed the exams and acquired liability insurance.

While my resume was somewhat fortified with education, the weakest element in my education was human anatomy. With time and continued study, I integrated anatomy into my classes and my sessions with clients. I was committed to staying on the injury-free side of this business, and I hoped the same would be true for my participants.

Perhaps one of the best things about acquiring these certifications is the connection between certification renewal and evidence of continuing education credits, CECs. These are easily attainable; usually a certain number of hours of learning are required, but yearly CEC accreditation simply isn't enough.

To be an excellent teacher requires a lifelong commitment to learning.

As a human being, staying open to new understandings supports openness to change.

Being open to change minimizes the tendency to become rigid or set in your ways.

CECs aside, it is vital to establish a balanced mindset: what you know today will continually need to be refreshed.

> If continuing education is to be part of your future, how can you ensure what you learn will both challenge you and, at the same time, fortify your teaching practice?
>
> If you have already entered this cycle, take a moment to reflect on your learning:
>
> > What professional development works for you financially and time-wise for your teaching practice.

Info Transfer

As an introvert who loves to learn, I could easily fall into the pattern of taking courses and continuing my education rather than stepping to the front of the stage to teach what I learned.

To counter this pattern, I tried to apply what I learned in a teaching situation as soon as I finished the course or the training.

I found my participants to be most supportive; I wasn't an expert, I was simply sharing what I had learned.

An example of an info transfer are my TRX and yoga sessions. I knew:

- There were no limitations so why not integrate yoga props into the TRX practice.

- My participants were comfortable with yoga asanas, all I needed to do was fuse yoga with the TRX.

- These sessions could be a blend of building strength and being relaxing.

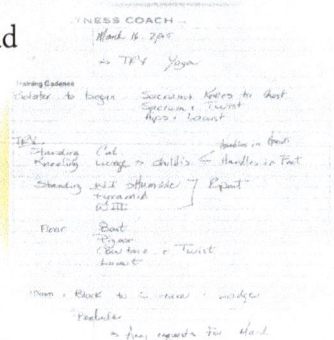

After you complete your next continuing credit course, enrich your learning by teaching it!

Gateway, not the way

*Some of us think holding on makes us strong.
But sometimes it is letting go.*

HERMAN HESSE

This business of yoga is very competitive. Classes are being offered in multiple venues by millions of different teachers who excel. You are now part of this competitive field.

Revenue from the business of yoga can be generated in numerous ways. Studios create flexible memberships based on payment per class, week, month or year. Private yoga classes create revenue with a drop-in fee or a registered session fee. Workshops, retreats, intensives and 30-day challenges add some revenue variety.

If this is to become your livelihood, you will need to make peace with teaching yoga and making money. You will also need to befriend competition, as it is ever present.

I finally landed a regular teaching spot at the fitness club where I was a member. As previously noted, the Sunday class was well attended; some days there would be twenty-four participants and some there would be seventy. I started to do the math. How much revenue would I generate if those same seventy participants came to a class I taught outside the club?

I was not prepared to make this leap of faith yet, but the seed had been planted.

If I were to do this, I would need to understand that my registration could fluctuate every week, just like the changing Sunday class size. In fact, I needed to embrace this possibility, because, to be honest, I loved working with those who came every week as much as I loved meeting and working with those new to my class.

I adopted a philosophy about commitment:

- I was committed to continually being a better teacher.

- The students I taught needed to be continually open to learning from other yoga teachers.

This philosophy would cause fluctuations in my business revenue. I would be, in a sense, encouraging my students to explore the world of yoga with *and* away from me. If I could solidify my philosophy, I would be setting the groundwork for both stability and instability in my future business.

When I look back at my teaching practice, this was the time I experimented with integrating different styles of yoga into my weekly class. Talking about a style of yoga before and during the class, opened their minds to the vast landscape of yoga. These were members of a fitness club, and yoga was becoming more accepted as an element of fitness, but the club would not be able to offer hot yoga or restorative yoga or aerial yoga.

Does it make sense to be a gateway, not the way?

I believed it did, as I continually enriched my life; seeking, learning, experiencing or revising.

As I reflect, I think I was not only building a teaching practice, I was building relationships. Lifelong relationships change as people move on, but those same relationships are beautiful when those paths cross again in the future.

In all the years I taught with this philosophy, I'm aware of only one person who left without ever wanting to cross paths with me again. I heard via the grapevine it was to do with my decision to change my venue—it was more affordable and less spacious. For some reason, this was off-putting for this person.

And that's okay… I was not the way.

> **What are your thoughts on competing for your piece of the yoga pie and, at the same time, understanding you may not be the way?**
>
> When you find your place in the yoga landscape, you may take business away from other yoga teachers.
>
> **How do you navigate the complexity of competition and yoga?**

Dueling Details

To be noticed or selected or chosen is contingent on many elements.

> *Some you can control, others are well beyond your control.*

I knew I could not compete for my place in the yoga world by being beautiful or funny or athletic or a good many other things.

But I could compete by being an exceptional teacher. All I needed was to be patient, diligently working on my preparation.

This resulted in hours of planning and mapping out yoga class sequences well in advance of my teaching schedule.

To those around me, it seemed like I was spending too much time. To me, it was exactly the right amount of time.

Take a look back at your planning history:

- What do your class plans reveal about your teaching place in the competitive world of the yoga business?

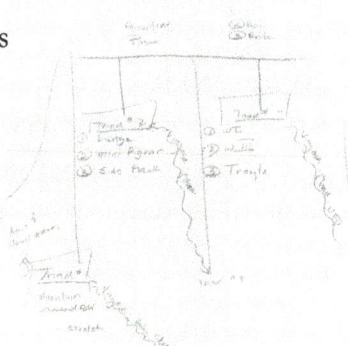

My way

Past is experience.
Present is experiment.
Future is expectation.
Use your experience in your experiments
to achieve your expectations!

AUTHOR UNKNOWN

The more I learned about teaching yoga, the more I attended to the subtle details of the world around me. I was definitely in sync with the concept of making yoga accessible and valuable to those skeptical or reluctant because of their perceived lack of flexibility. And then, when I wasn't expecting it, I heard another, very specific, call to teach.

I was in the Women's Only section of the club, working my way through my personal workout when I noticed a young male personal trainer enter with a woman in her early fifties.

When you have decades of experience as a member of a fitness club, you become fluent in assessing the new member's experiences with fitness. This woman was enthusiastic, likely a recent sign up with the bonus incentive of a couple of free training sessions.

How can you tell? Sometimes it's body composition, sometimes it's attire, but for me, especially with females, it's confidence. If I were to speculate, this woman was ready to prioritize her fitness, but she desperately hoped her fitness goals would arrive quickly and painlessly.

My guess was that she had very little experience with resistance or strength training, yet this young trainer led her straight to the TRX.

For those not familiar, the TRX is a suspension trainer that seems to attract the uber-fit. In reality, the TRX has the potential to work for all levels of fitness. It's also important to note, the TRX trainer is often suspended in high traffic areas, as was the case with this TRX scenario.

I was not tracking this vignette second by second…until I realized he had put her in a TRX plank—likely one of the more challenging exercises, one usually integrated after a certain level of fitness is achieved.

A TRX plank means hands on the floor, feet in the foot cradles. My low back ached just thinking about how this must feel for this woman. She gave it an honest effort for a mere five seconds. The coaching support she received was, "You can do more, your legs weren't even shaking!"

That could have easily been me if I had a different life situation where fitness didn't fit into my life. This was my mother's life situation. This was the reality for thousands, no millions of women: aspiring to being more fit, but never finding the right time or space.

I was already on my way to building a personal training element into my business plan, thus making way for my epiphany—you know those moments when you realize what you are seeking is right in front of you!

No, I didn't say anything to the woman or the trainer—it was none of my business—but I wondered how I could build a business specifically for menopausal or post-menopausal women with little or no fitness experience.

It was never my intention to be exclusive—the reluctant yogi was a vast group of fascinating men and women—but what if I could truly focalize my passion for the woman at this life stage?

This is an interesting phase of an emerging business: seeking the right type of client.

I wanted to attract the right clients, not necessarily a lot of clients.

Who are the right clients for your teaching practice?

Laws of Attraction

To attract the clients I had identified, I subtly weave elements of curiosity into the designs.

The practice unfolds into a series of explorations and discoveries resulting in my participants thinking less about how inflexible they are!

This means I also must remain curious.

- Sometimes I bring a prop to my planning mat, like the yoga strap, and ask myself, "How do I want to use this strap?"

The answers are sometimes yoga asanas, sometimes mobility exercises and sometimes unique patterns of movement. I'm delighted with my discoveries and I think that delight emerges when I teach.

Bring a prop of your choice to your mat:

- How many ways can you use this prop?

Design a practice based on your discoveries.

Master & Beginner

**A book is a magical doorway
to a world of adventure and possibility.**

UNKNOWN

Making money, making meaning

*Life shrinks or expands in
proportion to one's courage.*

ANAIS NIN

My regular Sunday morning yoga teaching gig continued to stretch me as a teacher, but the weekends seemed nonexistent as I was still spending a large portion of my leisure time creating practices and playlists as well as researching and rehearsing. I needed to create a better balance between my yoga teaching practice and my family-social life. It was time to think about transitioning out of this routine, time to analyze my current situation in preparation for a change.

From a revenue stream perspective, the club was paying me $27 per class. My monthly income, depending on the number of Sundays, was $108 per month. While not substantial, I wondered how could I generate that much, possibly more, each month?

When I make changes such as this, I proceed slowly to honor my personal pact: change forward. This means I'm committed to being where I am or where I'm going, not going back to where I've been. As I move forward, I metaphorically close the door behind me.

Teaching at yoga studios and other clubs was off the table. While the hourly or the class wage would likely be higher than what I was earning on Sundays, I wanted to experience the process of creating private classes that I promoted. I wanted to manage my schedule, my registrants, my expenses and my revenue on a very small scale.

I didn't want to create a treadmill of stress: running to stay ahead of time, space, money and energy. I already did that in my public teaching profession.

What I wanted was a space to teach a weekly yoga class. Just one space; just one class to call my own.

I started to pay attention to buildings in my neighborhood: churches, schools, community halls and empty retail spaces in malls. Then I created short lists for further investigation: select three spaces, go to their websites and inquire about a weekly evening rental space for 1.5 hours per week.

Many other groups and businesses had the same idea as I did. Some venues were indeed rented for yoga or fitness classes, but there were so many other interest groups running sessions in these community spaces. This small dream became less viable with each inquiry: no rental space, no weekly classes.

Finally, a bite.

A connection: someone I knew rented space at a nearby church, one I had not yet contacted.

The space was designated as a play-school during the day. As it was the only space that was available, I coordinated a time to view the space. If this had been my first tour, I would never have considered it. The reality was, there were few options available, so I had to use my imagination.

If I moved the tables and chairs into the breakout rooms, how many mats would fit?

The price was reasonable; the ambiance would need some work.

How would I know if I didn't try? I booked it and paid for a 6-week series.

Now I needed to promote my business and see how many registrants would follow me to this humble, non-yoga space.

> **Reflect on your vision for making meaning and making money:**
>
> What is your understanding of your current or potential revenue after expenses?
>
> How do you envision your marketing process to build enough interest in class registration?

Sky's the Limit

There is a visual art form present with all yoga postures. There are subtle layers of meaning, beyond the translation from Sanskrit, that can deepen the practice.

Much like the difference between doing yoga and practicing yoga, understanding the symbolism or the metaphors of yoga can deepen the practice.

For example, the eagle is considered to be the king of birds representing both power and victory due largely to their sharp vision.

I used this metaphor, sourced by another gem on my bookshelf called *Hatha Yoga The Hidden Language* by Swami Sivandanda Rahda, when I was asked to lead a yoga class for a group of elementary school teachers:

- **Supine Eagle**: what are your teaching aspirations?

- **Chair Eagle**: what limits your teaching potential?

- **Standing Eagle**: how can you sustain teaching excellence?

- **Prone Table Top Eagle** : open your heart, open your mind.

Do a bit of reading and select your own yoga pose and metaphor to build a practice around.

Small business or corporation

*You need to know off-balance
to achieve balance;
you need to become comfortable
with feeling off-balance
and slightly uncomfortable
with feeling balanced...
for surely something
will challenge your sense of stability!*

MY PRACTICE INTRO, OCTOBER 29, 2015

There were plenty of times I'd be lost in thought, walking or driving, when I questioned my sanity. Who did think I was at this point in my life and my career to veer off course, giving up employment stability for an untried and untested future career in yoga? Shouldn't I be settling into the well-worn treads leading women my age towards retirement?

Oh, I tried to convince myself to take the path most worn, and I may have done so if the local economy had stayed strong. Instead, an economic downturn shifted the scales of prosperity in real estate and businesses, so much so, the very educational small business I was employed by was downsizing. As the owners contemplated next steps, I contemplated my own.

Financially, this was not a perfect time to retire.

Business-wise, this was not a perfect time for self-employment. I had both my yoga and my personal training certifications, but only one weekly teaching position. I strategized two possible paths:

- Stay the course and see what contract the sports school would offer, given enrollment was trending downwards.

- Talk to my accountant and get her insights into establishing a company that was either a sole proprietorship or corporation.

After some contemplation and wise words from my accountant, I decided to form a corporation. I knew there could be potential corporate discounts if I decided to purchase equipment or props, plus my person and my personal property would be better protected if something were to derail towards a liability issue.

Finally, I was presented with an offer I could only refuse: the sports school offered a contract I was no longer interested in and the proposed salary was low enough to compete with a potential, meager revenue stream of my corporation.

As the saying goes, I jumped off the cliff. Quite a leap for me and for my family.

If I stayed the education route, discontentment would shape every aspect of my creative soul.

If I leapt, my only salvation would be my creative soul.

Heather Roselle became Your Fitness Coach Incorporated.

I was the owner of a business with the same address as my residence. There was no website, no social channel, no logo and the only revenue was my weekly yoga classes at the fitness club: $108 per month.

It sounds dramatic, but remember, I have been most fortunate in my life. This financial reality was buffered lovingly by the fact my spouse was still working, my son was living on his own and we did not have a mortgage.

The most dramatic element of this situation, aside from the fact I had no real clue what I was doing, was the fact I, for the first time since I was sixteen, did not have an incoming, regular pay cheque with my name on it: I was a dependent.

This was a sobering reality.

In some sense, it was an enlightenment of sorts; a first world enlightenment. I would learn to live without personal purchases for the time being.

My contentment increased exponentially.

My personal income decreased exponentially.

> **You are standing at the precipice: a career in yoga.**
>
> What are the potential risks?
>
> What are the potential rewards?

Life & Design

The longer I teach the more I am amazed by how life influences my designs.

If I am wrestling with something, it often finds its way into my class designs yet no one taking my class would know what I was wrestling with!

One such theme is the continual pattern of wanting a sense of stability but needing to increase mobility: to stay or to go. This theme lends itself beautifully to yoga class designs.

Consider creating a plan using this framework:

- Steadiness:

    What poses can flow using the wall as a prop?

- Mobile:

    What complimentary poses can flow from standing?

- Grounding:

    What poses can flow from prone position?

- Stillness:

    How can Savasana fortify this practice?

Intersection of commerce & person

*Great design is great complexity
presented via simplicity.*

M. COBANLI

My first rented space was not particularly relaxing or clean. It most certainly would not win any yoga studio design awards. But it was my place to explore being in the yoga business, my yoga business.

I had a portable speaker, a yoga mat and an iPod.

I purchased a Swiffer, dry cloths and a diffuser with an ambient light setting.

I set the number of spaces available at ten. There was potential for more, but I was already working with a simple space and I didn't want overcrowding.

My email promotion was intended to be personal. I wanted this group to know I was starting my yoga business, but I didn't want to sound desperate for their business. I had already found myself in similar situations over my lifetime; it is not comfortable to be a friend and a potential revenue or fundraising stream.

I also needed to think about the price per class.

If I considered the monthly membership fees at the club, the Sunday yoga class probably cost $1 per class if that member used all the facility had to offer. If I looked at the drop-in rate of yoga studios, it was about $12 per class, but the bundles of ten classes or unlimited monthly would cost significantly less than $12.

Truthfully, I didn't like this aspect of my business. Asking for money as payment for what I loved to do felt misaligned. But, I was responsible for generating an income for my personal life, and the only way I could do that was to start bringing revenue into my business.

I settled on $10 per class, but I decided to run this as a series rather than drop-in. Six weeks, $10 per class would equal $60 per registrant.

I received such support from this initial email. Words of encouragement were sent and, thankfully, there was enough interest to fill the space based on a maximum of ten participants.

Numbers and accounting are not my thing, but they needed to become my thing. I created class registration and check-in forms in Word, and I purchased a carbon copy receipt book for those who registered.

It's interesting to note, there were three registrants from the fitness club—the rest were men and women I knew personally.

The connections we make every day have the potential to become vital business connections for the future. Sometimes it's not the person you connect with but someone connected to them. Word does get out there and, in my case, it has been always what builds my business when I'm ready to grow, when my confidence is fortified to take the next steps.

If I'm alone, the place is more important.

If I'm sharing a space with others, the person is usually the most important thing.

There are times when both are of equal value.

It was this kind of thinking that allowed me to see the potential of my first rented space—I was focused on who would sign up rather than where I would teach.

Think about your experiences with *person* **and** *place*.

If both are present, a person and a place, which is most important to you?

Make a list of these examples.

Are there any exceptions?

If so, what are they?

How do person and place influence where you teach?

Simply Simple

In an effort to gain confidence as a yoga teacher, I would over plan to ease my discomfort.

But there were times when I needed to remind myself to simplify.

> *To simplify aligns with being present.*

On such occasions I would create a few invitations for myself:

- Find a quiet, calm space to practice.
- Set your timer for 12 minutes.
- Let your body create the sequence.
- Finish with a restorative pose and supportive props.

These practices were seldom recorded, shared or taught.

> *They were simple moments in time where I allowed myself to receive the gifts of my own teaching.*

> *I encourage you to do the same!*

Trial and error

*Our deepest fear is not that we are inadequate.
Our deepest fear is that we are
powerful beyond measure.
It is our light, not our darkness,
that most frightens us.*

MARIANNE WILLIAMSON

My humble play-school studio sessions were gaining traction—on a small scale, mind you, but I added another evening class on Mondays and increased the available mat space for both the Wednesday and the Monday classes. It was time for me to let go of my Sunday yoga class.

When it was my last class, I took a moment at the end to tell those present of this change. I didn't promote my private classes, I merely hinted that my search for other yoga teaching opportunities was the reason for leaving. I expressed gratitude for all I had learned teaching them and any other member who found their way to my Sunday yoga class. Some of the participants already knew what I was doing and likely shared the info when asked.

Although the Sunday class was not a huge revenue stream for me, it was a bit unnerving to let go of this security.

If my classes were growing in this church space, where were the other spaces to run my business? The best rent-free location was the lower level of my home space. This, of course, required discussion with my spouse, given the potential of clients coming into our home.

With a bit of reorganizing—60% of our basement level was already designated for fitness—my home studio had the potential to facilitate private and small group yoga and fitness sessions. No rental fees, just a contribution to the heating and electricity bills.

My home studio invited freedom to explore a series of creative trials, not all of which were sustainable or revenue rich!

Here are some of the highlights from my promotions:

Restorative Yoga - Futon mats

This had real wheels, or so I thought. The futon yoga mats were pricey but sumptuous. The price per mat was reasonable, but the currency exchange and shipping were not.

Some simple math:

> How many restorative yoga classes did I need to teach to justify the expense of purchasing four futon mats?

Most yoga studios were offering restorative classes. The props and blankets were shared, thus not desirable from a hygiene perspective given the number of uses related to the number of times they were cleaned or laundered.

I went for it. The futons arrived—they were outstanding, but a new problem emerged: where would I store them?

If you have ever owned a futon, you know they are heavy, not foldable or deflatable. Eventually, I found a solution, but each time I stored them, the futon mats became more and more like concrete.

The restorative yoga classes were not as viable as I predicted; about six clients remained committed to the restorative practice. This concept class worked best when offered monthly or every six weeks.

Sadly, the futons eventually were used elsewhere, then donated as I found a better product: Lotus Palm Thai yoga mats. These mats served a much greater purpose, plus they were easy to clean, store and use for yoga and fitness sessions.

TRX Yoga

One of my earliest purchases was the acquisition of four TRX and four ceiling anchors. My vision for this system was to add a novel element to yoga.

These classes were more viable than the restorative yoga classes because I could weave elements of yoga, resistance training and mobility into each session. The challenge was always space, but I could sequence and design based on the personalities that signed up.

It was interesting some years later to see TRX offering TRX yoga training certifications… I wasn't the only one who saw this potential!

Master Yoga Classes

Alright, the use of the word master is on the post *#metoo* block to be revised but in my world, it was a label that indicated deep study. I had some regular clients who loved to learn as much as I did. They inspired me to think of ways to keep them engaged—one such way was to offer private master classes. These were well-received due to my familiarity with the participants: they often shared a similar yoga experience while they mindfully expanded their repertoire and their love of the practice. We studied specific asanas and the use of a multitude of props to enrich their home practice.

Luxury Stay-cation Retreats

While I often dream of traveling to a tropical yoga retreat, I confess to being a homebody. Travel has never been an interest or a passion, but staying in local, luxury accommodations is one of my special treats.

Yoga retreats were coming on strong. Most of the local studios were offering them, in a variety of locations, as were the yoga celebrities of the time. Some were natural, organic or rustic, and others were luxurious, tropical or spa-like.

I wondered: could I create a luxury retreat that would fall into the stay-cation category?

I did exactly what I did when I was looking for a yoga space to rent. This time I paired up with my sister-in-law, partly because I love her company and partly because she has good taste.

We narrowed our property search to two hotels in the downtown area. One was an eclectic art-themed hotel called Hotel Arts; the other was a new boutique hotel property called Le Germain.

When we had a tour of Hotel Arts, it was a modestly-renovated Holiday Inn. Sure, it had charm, but the ambiance didn't capture the spirit we were seeking.

Then we toured Le Germain. It was new, shiny and very upscale. The assistant manager was easy to chat with and saw the potential of a yoga retreat. We committed to this location and started the negotiations for the hotel's first yoga retreat.

It was easy to map out the weekend: a perfect mix of yoga, mingling, relaxing and socializing. The challenge was cost. The hotel had a bottom line; we were new on the retreat scene. A commitment was made to go for it, knowing there would be little or no revenue for Your Fitness Coach Inc.

I loved the entire process of creating, promoting, managing and delivering.

Those first participants were pampered and pleased with their experience.

On the accounting side, the total revenue after expenses was around $60.

The tough sell was the price tag: everyone knew it was cheaper to go to Mexico than it was to stay close to home.

Still, the interest was there.

We ran a second retreat and then tried to run a third in Montreal. This was a hotel chain from the province of Quebec, so why not add a cultural component? The third promotion did not yield enough interest, so sadly, we let that concept go.

In between these weekend retreats, we also tried running Le Germain Yoga & Brunch classes—Sundays were quiet and parking was free. The studio was on the eleventh floor, surrounded by windows. We had a yoga practice, then went to the dining room for brunch. This was well-received and accessible for all wanting to take part.

Yoga & Guitar

As previously mentioned, music plays a large role in both the creation and delivery of my yoga practices. I am blessed to have a musically gifted son who was willing to join me on this adventure.

The premise of this trial was to blend live classical guitar music with my practice. We promoted this concept in a variety of ways: a special Christmas promotion at the fitness club, aligning the event with a seasonal solstice, opening night of a Le Germain yoga retreat, a New Year's Day practice and finally, whenever my son was available.

The preliminary concept was to add value to the yoga experience. The long game was to record the music, which would become revenue for my favorite musician. It still sits on an idea page with potential for digital downloads in the future.

Karma Classes

Of all my business explorations, karma classes are my favorite. I don't get paid, the money I collect is paid forward to select charities.

The way I structured these classes was to promote a karma class, collect the registration fee and then, as the participants entered the space, ask that they put their name and the name of a charity on a piece of paper.

Depending on the number of registrants, my goal was to match the registration pot from my business. If the group registration generated $100, Your Fitness Coach paid $100 resulting in a donation of $200.

When the class ended, I would draw the name of one registrant and the name of their charity. A cheque was mailed and we all left with a bit more joy than when we arrived.

Silent Auction

I was enamored with the concept of yoga and guitar. Not just for more time with my son, but for more layers of sensory experiences when fusing live music with yoga. There were opportunities to promote Yoga & Guitar with several silent auctions for local charities.

If your vision is to own a studio or to be more like a consultant, your imagination will be a constant companion.

It's your business, however large or small, so make it what you want it to be, rather than what it's supposed to be or what every other business is.

There will be hits and there will be misses…before even considering them, let your imagination run free:

What ideas could be converted to revenue streams?

Once your list is complete, keep it alive by revisiting it quarterly, updating it whenever the muse hits!

Keep it Light

With so many ideas and trials, your yoga preparation may take some interesting turns.

The more you read and research, the more ideas you will generate...with plenty of joyful moments in-between.

I went through a foot fitness research and learning phase, integrating my growing understanding of foot anatomy into my class designs.

It was awesome, so much so I created a plan called Toe-tally Awesome:

- Standing meditation with toe awareness.
- Mountain, crescent lunge and triangle with foot connection awareness.
- Supine hand to big toe with rotations.
- Savasana with relaxed feet.

Start to play with words, asanas, research and your ongoing evolution as a yoga teacher to keep it light and inspirational.

For you.

For your participants.

*You're not here to be average, you're here to be **awesome!***

Power of voice

Noticing. What a gift.

BYRON KATIE

I am fascinated by speech patterns. I listen to the language of film, big and small screen, to better understand the characters. When I'm out and about, I listen to conversations: tone, phrasing, lingo—of children, teens and adults. If I'm reading fashion or entertainment magazines, I look for trendy phrases…and I try not to fall into patterns of language that simply fill a silent space in a conversation.

Yoga teachers utilize language to connect with a class, cue a practice and allow for silent spaces somewhere in between.

Personally, I am very comfortable with silent spaces; I have never needed to fill space with dialogue and yet, I love to be with others whose rich conversation fills those very empty spaces. Whether you're a talker or a listener, listening to your own words when you teach will continually inspire you to expand your vocabulary or add variety to often used transition phrases…*like, so, um, you know, right, and more.*

When cuing a class, the purpose of words is to move the body through a practice, especially in cases where Sanskrit is not used. I have caught myself using repeater words and phrases.

There are a lot of them in yoga:

- Just breathe.

- Find your center.

- Take a vinyasa.

- Move into downward facing dog.

- Relax.

- Be present.

To minimize repetition and maximize the power of language, it is valuable to set aside time to analyze your patterns of speech, and then do some vocabulary or phrasing enhancement.

What are the most common phrases you hear while taking a yoga class?

What are common phrases you've heard yourself speak in conversation or teaching?

If you are comfortable, record yourself teaching. Analyze and then rework the script.

Find ways to enrich your language.

What are other words or phrases you overuse?

One of my favorite language conditioning resources is a thesaurus, book form.

If I hear myself over using a word like calm, I go to the thesaurus to remind myself of similar but different words…peace, serene, settle, ease, gentle, tranquil, pause, still.

Language Refresh

To know is one thing.

To change is a completely different process!

You have taken some time to **hear** yourself talk.

Now it's time to intentionally enhance your language patterns:

You say...	You could say...

Yoga fashion-ations

*Your body is a temple;
your mind is the door.*

AUTHOR UNKNOWN

I have long been fascinated by fashion, the influences on how people dress personally and professionally. When I was teaching, I was intrigued by the challenge of not looking like a teacher. This is not intended to be an insult to the profession, but there were stereotypes that existed for female teachers.

It was fascinating to re-experience these observations as I moved towards becoming a yoga teacher. Yoga images and yoga celebrities do not wear many layers of clothing—for very good reason: layers of clothing distract from feeling the sensations of the body within a practice. When I practiced my yoga, I wore the same close-fitting yoga attire that was fashionable for that time.

I noticed yoga had become sexy: it was in vogue and photographed much like fashion. Like Jack Johnson, surfer/singer/songwriter, I called it *sexy plexy*. Sexy plexy was not part of my fashion wheelhouse, and it most certainly would not be part of my yoga teacher image.

While I saw the aesthetic of beauty and sexuality in yoga, I did not need that level of distraction, given I already was often distracted by calming my nerves before teaching.

Seems like a silly dilemma, but nonetheless, a significant one for me.

It took some thinking and a bit of shopping, but I landed on an image that worked for me:

- Black leggings, no fabric restrictions—especially around the waist.

- Tank with a shelf bra, contrasting color, no restrictions.

- Light, long-sleeved crew neck t-shirt; short sleeve t-shirt for warmer rooms.

- Vibram shoes.

I always pay for excellent quality leggings, tanks and Vibrams…the t-shirts are picked based on breathability and comfort for practice.

No bare arms, no cleavage, no navel, no back…not even my feet were exposed. It worked for me. When I see bare arms, cleavage, navels, backs, arms and more, in a yoga setting or otherwise, I merely admire the human body and that person's comfort in their own skin. No judgment, just a distinction. My look is more modest, aligning with my inner self to not draw attention to myself.

A quick note about the Vibrams. Bare feet and yoga are synonymous, but I was never comfortable walking anywhere but my own house in bare feet. As I gained teaching comfort, trusting my cuing more and my yoga demonstrations less, I found wearing Vibrams provided a yoga mat on my feet wherever I happened to be. They still work for me to this day. Did anyone notice all this attention to my professional yoga attire?

There have been a few times when I have been complimented for looking professional, and I appreciated the observation, as I continually take time to think about what professional looks like the longer I teach. Remember, my niche is 40+, mostly women. I suspect different compliments are shared with other yoga teachers with an alternate view.

> **What are your observations, not judgments, about yoga teaching attire and professionalism?**
>
> What is your image, or what are you exploring with the image you put out there—you, the yoga teacher?
>
> What are the layers that work for you?

Random Landing

Every so often I explore the marvelous human body using chakras as a framework.

In many instances, I have sequenced a class using asanas that align from the root to the crown chakras.

There have been other times when a season, like Christmas holidays, infuses the need for most humans to quietly connect to the present tense.

One such year, the word *embrace* emerged as a theme. It seemed random but it was perfect for the participants at that particular point in time.

Try following these leads to see where your idea finds a random, but meaningful landing:

- Refresh and update your understanding of chakras.
- How does the calendar date influence which chakras shape your design?
- Is there a word or a concept that emerges as a possible umbrella for this practice?

Let your class design emerge.

When the shoe just doesn't fit

*Give a woman the right shoes and
she can conquer the world.*

MARILYN MONROE

Like so many, I continually face the very things I avoid the most. Introverts are private, so sharing what I do in my business has been a perennial challenge. Additionally, I've struggled with accounting. Self-promotion and accounting are essential when building a business, especially when you are the only human in charge of that business!

If only I could just teach yoga or run retreats or coach fitness without promoting, accounting or communicating—a pure fantasy. Over the last ten years, I have experimented with different ways to communicate, promote and account.

There is an endless supply of how-to-build-your-business resources out there. This is a vast world where confident and successful, usually extroverted, individuals share their business success secrets. If you decide to tap into the wisdom of Internet success and acclaim, put your mind on high filter to avoid the slippery learning slope. It doesn't take long before you find yourself enraptured by the wisdom of some successful person living your dream. At first, the wisdom is generously shared, but there is always a payback point: a purchase, a like, a subscription or an invitation to join the email community. I was appreciative of many pearls of wisdom I collected, yet this research process continually reminded me of what I didn't, and still don't, like about marketing and promotion.

One thing became evident: every business is unique to itself; every business owner must create a code that works for both the owner and clients. My code, now part of my corporate year-end, is simple:

- What's working?

- What needs to improve?

- What do I need to invest in to improve?

Communication & Promotion

In the beginning, I utilized my personal email to communicate and promote my classes. These email messages were sent about four weeks in advance until a problem emerged: as the number of recipients in the group increased, my messages were more often identified as spam. At this very same time, I noticed crisp email messages from other businesses coming into my mailbox. Constant Contact and MailChimp seemed to be the most common email applications being used by reputable businesses.

If I subscribed to such a service:

- Would my communications look more interesting?

- More importantly, would my email be delivered to inboxes rather than junk folders?

- What was the cost per month or year for these subscriptions?

> How complicated was the process of transferring my contacts?

> Would the privacy of my contact list be ensured?

After in-depth research and reflection, I settled on Constant Contact. I could create a template with my logo, and add links and images. My messages looked more professional.

This mode of communicating remained in place until my business shifted direction again, moving towards private yoga and fitness. Now my contact list was smaller, but those on the list were what I call *frequent flyers*.

I cancelled my Constant Contact subscription and went back to using my personal email.

Accounting

Accounting was still an area I kept in a dark corner of my workspace. I began using Word for my record keeping: manual receipt templates were emailed; monthly tabulations for expenses and revenue were documented in a Word table using a calculator. It was not efficient, but I was comfortable accounting with this hands-on approach.

As is always the case, the moment of truth came: this so-called hands-on approach wasn't working. I was simply avoiding learning more about accounting software and spreadsheets!

Back to my research…what was the best software for a small business like mine?

At that time, MindBody was the new software on the yoga and fitness scene. It was visually appealing, relatively accessible to learn and, for the first year, the cost aligned perfectly with my business.

When I switched to this application, collecting fees also became easier. Now my clients could pay by credit card, cheque, e-Transfer or cash. The software produced helpful reports on revenue streams and individual clients.

When the time came to renew my subscription, MindBody was a global success, and small businesses like mine were no longer a good fit due simply to the increased cost to subscribe. I cancelled my subscription and rebooted my search for accounting software.

Square arrived on scene, targeting small businesses like mine. I purchased a portable tap for payments on-site, but I still needed something for my accounting and invoicing purposes.

Zero is excellent accounting software, highly compatible with Apple computers. The only issue was Zero connected with PayPal and Stripe, but not with Square.

Square just keeps getting better; more in-tune with what small businesses need. The company eventually offered an invoicing service. Now I just use SquareUp to send invoices, accept payments and send receipts.

It's simple.

It works.

I have no regrets for taking so long to find the right product for me, my business and my clients. Again, mine is a small business, so I could manage the inefficiencies until I needed something better.

Websites and Socials

My final frontier: learning how to have a digital presence other than my live stream Zoom classes!

Truthfully, I'm still dragging my heels on this one.

This is an even more vast world where more confident and more successful—and usually extroverted—individuals share their success secrets.

Another slippery slope. It doesn't take long before you find yourself enraptured by the wisdom of some successful person with a million or more followers living their dream. At first, the wisdom is generously shared, but there is an always a payback point: a purchase, a subscription, an invitation to join the email community. It simply reminded me of what I didn't and still don't like about having a digital presence! But, I surrendered and entered the world of trial and error.

I tried GoDaddy…easy to set up, a reasonable price. After one year, I saw my business revenue was generated by my email promotions, not my website. GoDaddy was cancelled.

I tried WordPress…a supposedly easy to set up website with reasonable prices. I never really felt confident with this platform. After another year of not using this, I cancelled.

I tried SquareSpace…my longest relationship with a website. I admit to loving this company as a website builder. The support videos are excellent and whenever I've encountered a problem, the technical support has been both efficient and helpful but the company did not align its payment options with Square.

Finally, I set-up a simple website with Square. It suits the nature of my business.

Social channels? Facebook and Instagram just really didn't fly with me. I tried to post on both for a while, but I didn't fit that universe. I still don't.

TikTok is a no-go zone for me.

I have been drawn into these social channels by beautiful, talented, energetic and creative humans, then grown increasingly annoyed with myself for wasting time watching them. I challenged myself to re-assess my network by asking the question:

- How does this channel add value to my person, my place and my profession?

This was a powerful exercise, the end of which resulted in the silencing of most notifications. I still give myself the challenge—and maintain it to this day—of checking Facebook and Instagram once a day. My max time on socials is less than ten minutes per day, usually five minutes or less, for the following:

- Facebook has some personal and some professional notifications on my news feed; I feel connected to what's going on, but not immersed in it.

- Instagram is mostly for my family and close friends.

When I think about adding my business to these channels, I do not believe it aligns with who I am or my clients. Yet, I have much respect for those who have built a business this way.

As a good friend often says, "You do you, I'll do me."

With a mind curious, not competitive or critical, explore your relationship with the Internet and socials:

Thinking about categories, who do you follow or like: family, friends, interests, education, other?

Thinking about your routine, when do you connect to the Internet or socials?

Thinking about your preferences, name one person, business or group that stands out in your feed and then reflect on why.

How can I Help

I frequently remind myself to enjoy the moments with my participants...life unexpectedly pulls them in different directions for many important reasons.

As a result, they often express a desire to learn how to practice on their own.

The desire is there.

Sometimes they find themselves on their mats.

But this is where the challenge presents itself when they wonder, "What should I do?"

I have created a couple of workshops to build both confidence and a framework for a yoga home practice using anatomy and mat locations.

When you think about your current or prospective participants:

- What are two simple categories you could use to assist with building their home practices?

Never say never

Never say never because limits, like fears, are often just an illusion.

MICHAEL JORDAN

I have never enjoyed being in front of something…a stage, a camera, a video. Our family photo albums evidence this to be true.

When the pandemic arrived in 2020 and in person sessions were cancelled, I seriously considered closing the business and entering retirement, perhaps to fulfill my ever-present, ambitious drive to return to my writing.

But, two important women in my tribe asked me to consider doing virtual classes. My initial response was a firm no; holding to that position would mean closing the business.

When the reality of COVID hit, and we were in for the long haul of isolation, I realized I was not ready to close the business. I was not ready to quit teaching.

So, I reconsidered.

I agreed to give virtual teaching a try. What I knew was I would not record and post my teaching; I would do live stream classes for those interested.

The most important consideration was to find a platform that would provide the most privacy and allow for the most professionalism. I selected Zoom.

Because I questioned my ability to teach this way, I put together a trial schedule: one month of free classes to see if the Zoom studio would work for me and for those interested.

What a vast range of responses I received!

Some responded with the same fears I had…they were nervous about being in front of a camera too!

Some responded almost too lightheartedly…indicating they were not interested, and I sensed they doubted my ability to pull this off.

Some didn't respond at all… they had already moved towards YouTube, Peloton and other streaming options.

This was a new group dynamic and a new teaching frontier.

I wasn't the only one who needed to learn lighting, sound, camera angles and more, so I went back to the Internet—finding professional channels to learn from. Keeping my expenses low, I pulled together some suitable lighting options and tried various camera angles for my teaching space. The first two weeks of classes were challenging:

> I had issues connecting to twenty participants with a stable Internet connection; a WiFi booster helped.
>
> I had issues creating the right lighting; ring lights helped.

- I had issues seeing everyone in the gallery; I switched from my iPad to a laptop, and then eventually to a desktop.

- I had issues seeing everyone, even when I used a laptop or a desktop; I learned how to mirror my computer to a large, older TV.

After a few weeks, I had a new place to teach. The only place I could teach with the lockdown protocols. And I was loving the connections I made with my tribe from the comforts of my favorite place: home!

When in person classes and sessions resumed, I decided to stay virtual. Some of my participants went back to studios and classes, knowing they were welcome to drop back in if ever they wanted (remember: gateway, not the way).

Those who stayed continue to express appreciation for using their own props, being at home and remaining connected to an amazing tribe…they still love to see each other when we sign on. It's almost as if Zoom is novel because everything is moving back to normal.

I never would have imagined this is where I would be as my business recognizes its ten-year anniversary!

I've traveled a short distance with many amazing detours along the way.

When you think about yourself and yoga, do you have something you'd *never* consider?

You may never need to.

> In my case, I never wanted to be photographed or videotaped...my preference is to remain behind the camera or what I call backstage.
>
> I was comfortable being there.
>
> Until I was backed into the corner of either getting on the Zoom stage or leaving my business behind.

Why do you think this is the one thing you would not consider...

Leap of Faith

My first Zoom yoga class.

Super uncomfortable...yet thrilled to have the opportunity to teach when life as we knew it took a pandemic pause.

The women joining me were patient.

The practice was simple...all that was needed was a mat and a wall.

I did not expect myself to be perfect.

> *I expected myself to be prepared.*

I wasn't perfect.

> *I was prepared.*

When you are faced with a challenge:

- How do you prioritize your focus to ensure you are prepared for what you must face?

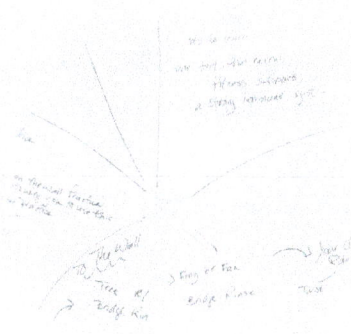

Who's driving the bus

I may not have gone where I intended to go,
but I think I have ended up where I intended to be.

DOUGLAS ADAMS

As I look back, I realize that having a business plan is like having reserved space at the back of the bus. From this position, the business can see who fills the seats, the road behind and the road ahead.

When I started, I knew nothing about writing a business plan and discovered an entire universe on how to write business plans. If you have a background in business, this would be a natural place to begin.

But my background was teaching. Teachers are required to draft and submit long-range teaching plans at the start of the year. The process was beneficial, serving as a road map for the year, although I don't remember revisiting the long-range plan as the year progressed, suggesting the process provided merely a sense of direction. Ultimately, the students I taught became the actual plan.

The value in being student-focused, as opposed to curriculum-focused, is the fusion of art and craft. It made little sense to plough through curricular objectives if the students were not ready to move on. The teaching-learning magic was discovered somewhere between the person and the curriculum within a time and space.

When it came time to put my business into a similar form, and draft a business plan like my teaching long-range plans, it made sense to align my vision with my year-end goal to generate revenue.

Therein lies the conflict that remains ever present.

It still doesn't feel natural to think of revenue before teaching or coaching. But, the reality is I am not a charitable organization; I am in business. Although the business supports an already comfortable life, I still need to demonstrate this is a legitimate business when I submit my year-end accounting documents.

It seemed somewhat grounding to focus on my clients. The group of mostly women and a few good men who signed up for sessions and classes.

With this focus, I identified two groups of clients:

- The clients who, for the most part, were working full-time with family responsibilities.

- The clients who, for the most part, were retired with family responsibilities and aspirations to travel.

This is an oversimplification, but these were my two revenue streams. My sessions and my classes needed to align with the interests and the availability of these two groups.

For those with daytime employment commitments, I asked for feedback regarding days and times of the week that worked best for a weekly yoga class. Over time, we settled on evening classes starting at 7pm, but the day of the week fluctuated depending on the availability of space and the lifestyle patterns of the group. Mondays worked for a while, then Wednesdays worked for a while as did Thursdays. These classes were always packaged as a series, usually six or eight weeks. This time frame seemed to accommodate the changes that aligned with everyone's vacations, travel and life.

For those with a more dynamic schedule, I ran classes on Wednesday and Friday mornings. The series still runs for six to eight weeks, but each woman sends her reservations based on her availability. I, in turn, create a schedule based on those reservations. The agreement remains: the class schedule aligns with a minimum enrollment of 4-6 students per class. This concept continues to work today with my live stream classes.

It's important to remember, this is a small business. A micro-business. A passion. I don't know how this could work for a similar business with higher overhead expenses like leased space. I rented spaces that were economical, not necessarily studio-quality, thus my overhead remained low, giving me a bit of freedom to individualize.

To keep my business fresh and my expenses low, I still maintain my teaching goal to not teach or coach the same sequence twice, and I remain open to requests and suggestions from those still taking my classes.

Ten years, a minimum of two classes per week is a lot of teaching.

As far as an annual plan goes, I do reflect each year, sometimes in a Word document, but more often now with a blank canvas. I have a month-end routine and a year-end routine; there are annual renewals and fees.

The tribe drives my bus.

Sometimes I'm not certain I can provide what they are asking for, but I am certain the journey to do so will keep me engaged!

It is essential to understand the elements of a good business plan.

It's even more important to create the essentials of the business you plan to grow.

Study how to create a business plan and make a list of your best resources.

Select the elements most valuable to you and your vision for your business and record the framework.

As you move forward, how will you keep monthly and annual records for your business history…a record of your seat at the back of the bus!

Around we go

Whether planning yoga class designs or creating my version of a business plan, I have used computers, unlined paper, lined paper, notebooks and applications.

One of the most brilliant planning designs I discovered was the circle.

It created a sense of taking a journey; a journey with both a starting and an ending point.

Take a look back at your design and planning creations:

- Is there a format you use more frequently than any other?
- Is there a format you haven't experimented with?
- How do your planning formats inform your business and your teaching practice?

  How might they provide insights into your history?

  How might they inspire designs for the future?

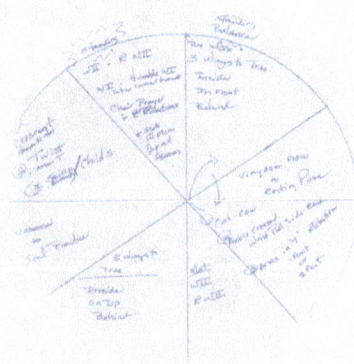

Is it really yoga

*You have to color outside the lines
if you want to make your life a masterpiece.*

ALBERT EINSTEIN

When I began this journey, I wanted to learn as much about yoga as I could. The history, the progressions and the evolution of this ancient practice.

My learning would be constructed and understood based on my location in life: I was middle-aged; I was a seasoned classroom teacher, but I was an infant in my yoga studies.

Because learning is continuous, I have learned so much more than yoga: body rolling, mobility sticks, yoga walls, aerial yoga, fascial fitness, Thai Yoga Massage, foam rollers and more. What I teach now might be better named MOBA or MOBY.

I am still inspired by Shiva Rea and Sage Rountree, but also by Yamuna, Jill Miller and their world of self-care; by Bernie Clark for his world of yin with a Canadian flavor; Ryder Carroll for modernizing analog thinking and planning; and Thomas Myers for new understandings of human anatomy.

All these teachers and more continue to infuse my practice. I model learning when I teach by sourcing my inspiration; I plant seeds for others to learn. The journey others take with regard to their learning may not be for the purpose of teaching, but for the purpose of better understanding their bodies as they change and mature.

Innovation arises when passion meets a roadblock… at least that is how my yoga teaching practice has evolved. The most innovative leaders in yoga and fitness apply the foundations of practice to create a new version, hence the branding and rebranding of new ways to move the human body.

> **Make a list of roadblocks you are currently facing or anticipate facing:**
>
> **Select three roadblocks for deeper study.**
>
> > How might each of these roadblocks be converted to an innovative path?

Openly Creative

I have always brought yoga props and mobility tools to my in-person classes.

When I shifted to live stream, I was able to encourage my participants to purchase props and gear for their home practice.

These were small investments:

- Bender balls
- Tune-up balls
- Soft foam rollers
- Bolsters and more

These investments are a regular element of my class designs...I aim to keep these props dust-free by integrating them into my virtual classes.

If I look back through my notes, I can easily see when it's time to bring out a certain prop.

I often plan with this prop by simply asking myself, "What yoga asanas can we do with this?"

- Give it a try... bring a prop to your next design session and see what you can create.

Tools of the trade

Knowing others is intelligence.
Knowing yourself is true wisdom.
Mastering others is strength.
Mastering yourself is true power.

LAO TZU

All artists and craftspeople utilize tools of their trade. These tools can organize, reorganize, update, refresh and redesign; all of which infuse novelty into your practice. Here are some of the sources I've accessed to update my teaching toolbox.

Yoga Streaming

Streaming classes were an evolving concept before the global pandemic. The marketing targeted what I was looking for: access to a variety of virtual yoga classes that I could do from home.

The beginning of a subscription was exceptional. It seemed like a vast library of teaching styles and teachers, but the novelty wore off within 6-8 weeks; it seemed the teachers that appealed to me the most had a limited number of videos.

For me, change is essential. Repetition is beneficial in small doses. This is how I'm hardwired, so these subscriptions were cancelled at the onset of decreased interest.

Training & Certifications

Continuing education credits are essential to support ongoing professional development. Because I was required to submit these as part of my annual certification renewals, I looked beyond the convenient courses, which meant I was seeking learning opportunities that far exceeded the minimum hours of education required each year. I looked for education that would enhance my business, my coaching and my teaching.

I immersed myself in a body of work by Yamuna Zake, traveling to Seattle, then finding a local certified teacher to continue my studies.

As well as:

- a virtual course, *On A Roll* by Jill Miller
- intensive Thai Yoga Massage by a local massage therapist
- Yin Teacher Training by a local Yin Yoga specialist
- Aerial Yoga offered at a local yoga studio
- TRX Suspension training for group exercise
- Online TRX Yoga training

Self-Directed Study

I remind myself that I am a teacher with an undergraduate and masters degree in education plus nearly twenty years of classroom experience—I can teach myself as well as I can teach others.

Like most things, the cost of doing business and living continues to become more expensive. The same is true for training, certifications and courses.

I had Yoga Nidra teacher training on my wishlist for some time. During the global pandemic, there were several excellent Nidra teachers offering virtual teacher training. To be honest, I found the registration fees beyond what I was willing to pay—my own revenue was down substantially, which was another reason for my hesitation.

I looked at the body of published books on Yoga Nidra, created a mini business plan and opted to purchase four books for my self-directed study.

The cost of these books was $125.00; the cost of the training was $1,200.00.

Then I offered monthly free Nidra classes to gain some experience fusing the concepts into my teaching practice. If you want to learn something well, teach it!

While I will not be able to use these books for CECs, or to claim I am a certified Nidra teacher, I have taken the knowledge and woven it into the fabric of the clients I work with in a class called Bliss Yoga.

This complimentary class was created based on the feedback from my clients who often expressed how much they enjoyed the feeling of fusing meditation with Savasana. I shifted some of the Nidra sequencing to language based on what I knew or sensed was going on in their lives. Bliss

Yoga became a peaceful reset to sleep better, breathe better or simply minimize worrying with a repeating mantra: "You are here…the only place you can be."

This has led me to learn a new application, Adobe Audition, and to learn how to use an external microphone for my voice. I have created a small recording studio (under my stairs) and a handout to support a home practice. Going forward, I hope to fuse music into these scripts—my Bliss Yoga teaching will remain a gift for those interested.

Building a Personal Library

Having books at my fingertips has been invaluable. Every year, I review my shelves: books that no longer provide inspiration are given to someone in my tribe to create space for new books.

I also have a virtual bookshelf, e-books I have purchased for portability and convenience. Having both a physical and virtual library is the heart and soul of my inspiration for teaching.

Bullet Journal

Since being introduced to Ryder Carroll, I have rekindled my fondness for pen and paper. The Bullet Journal has sparked a vast business of paper products…blank, lined, grids and dots; large, small, coils, staples; and writing tools.

As mentioned, I started my yoga teaching journey with a large sketchbook in hand and to this day, I still have notebooks in hand. Much of my creativity begins with pen and paper. Dotted paper: small coil notebooks, large stapled notepads and everything in-between.

Creating new plans every class created a new problem—what to do with these sketchbooks? When the time came to convert the notes into this book, I selected the pages with plans I deemed to be most novel, connected them by year and then recycled the rest.

Digital Detours

When the notebooks started to create space issues, I dabbled with creating practices using Word, then Illustrator, then InDesign. The issue for me was file management. I never felt as connected to my electronic files as I did to my paper...until I came across a writing application called Ulysses.

Ulysses

This application for writers operates much like email, allowing for space to write and folders to organize.

Today, all my creations are drafted in Ulysses, but when I teach, I convert my notes onto a small whiteboard that remains visible to me throughout the class—the whiteboard is photographed before being erased then attached to the file.

If I want to look at my past practices, I simply open the yoga folder; if I want to explore the last time I taught a Yin style class, I search using the word "Yin".

This application allows for photographs and notes; I take pictures of the visuals to help me remember and assist in capturing a moment in history. Visuals can be my whiteboard notes, quotes or illustrations, or my paper notes if I used them.

The beauty of Ulysses is all my files can be converted to Word, ePUB or rich text files if I want to use them in an alternate way.

It's been a game changer for my preparation, my creativity and my organization.

Paper still has value to me, but when I finish with a page, I take a photograph and attach it to the Ulysses file. Paper is continuously recycled, but the content is always accessible.

Music

When I taught my in-person classes, I created a playlist to support each practice. For some, the connection to the music was continuous, for others, the music became background.

Learning to create, name and organize my playlists creates a simple history.

The challenge with virtual classes on Zoom is sound quality. I no longer weave music into the planning but hope, as I explore the concept of portability with my business, I can find a way to share my playlists for others to use when they practice…inspiring them to create their own.

All professions have essential tools—tools, of course, being metaphorical or literal.

Make a list of your most reliable tools:

Make a wishlist of tools you will explore in the future:

Music Infusion

Of all the tools, music remains a powerful source of design inspiration.

Pick one of your favorite playlists or design one for today or select one from my archives.

Once you have set your ambiance, your mat and your volume, allow the music to unite with your creativity and your intuitive understanding of yoga.

Follow the flow.

Finish in Savasana.

Never easy

*The influence of a good teacher
can never be erased.*

AUTHOR UNKNOWN

As I near the end of this collection, I am still very much in awe of the fact that teaching, even after all these years, has not become easy or natural.

It remains quest-like:

- How much more can I learn from the process?

- How much more can I improve what I say, what I do, how I plan, how I reflect?

Yet, during this quest, there is a creative process that is greatly supported by my planning tools and my discipline.

When the time comes to prepare, the challenge is the same: I question whether I can come up with yet another new practice plan.

Sometimes it's a word or a theme or a page from a book that meets my Ulysses workspace.

But life is filled with surprises and changes so I count on them for creation-connection points.

I plan from my mat, often with a book selected from my shelf. As the design takes shape, I capture the ideas using Ulysses. The rehearsal, my personal practice, becomes a flow, and then the words for the Savasana or the mediation surface. I am no longer distracted by nervousness as I know exactly who is joining my class.

Instead of traveling to teach, I move to the comforts of my home studio at the scheduled time.

Sure, there are details that would make my space better, but my focus remains on those beautiful smiling faces that enter the Zoom waiting room. I am inspired to teach more when I experience my plan coming to life, virtually, with participants comfortably practicing from their home studios.

We connect.

We practice.

We conclude in a space called Savasana.

At the end, I never tire of expressing my gratitude for each and every one of these amazing women who take time out of their demanding lives to practice with me.

Teaching is both a privilege and a gift.

I am most fortunate to have been on this teaching path for thirty-six years; from the classroom to the sports school to my current business.

I remain inspired to teach and appreciate the monetary rewards that follow…but mostly, I appreciate the opportunity to explore the artistry that is integral to the teaching process.

You are here...time has shifted.

You are different now than you were when we started, the path ahead is as mysterious as ever.

> How will what you know today shape where you go tomorrow?

Repeat Treat

Treat yourself by signing up for a yoga class with a gifted yoga teacher.

When you arrive on your mat, release your expectations and allow yourself to be a learner, a learner open to receive the gifts from yoga and from the teacher.

After the class, give yourself as much time as your day allows to let that teacher and that class settle into your soul.

No notes.

No redesign.

No reflection.

The last word

*When you love what you have,
you have everything you need.*

AUTHOR UNKNOWN

I do not consider myself to be an expert or leader in the field of teaching, business or yoga.

I believe and remind myself daily that I have more to learn than what I already know.

I accept there may be elements of this book that are irrelevant to you, but I hope those irrelevancies are converted into something meaningful.

I understand there are many who receive monetary gains from yoga and I applaud this ability to mesh making meaning with making money.

I am convinced the world needs more yoga to better understand where we are and the multitude of directions possible for where we need to go—united, connected, generous, accepting, supportive.

I hope this book has made a small difference in your journey.

The last words are yours.

Finish these phrases:

I do not consider myself…

I believe and remind myself daily…

I accept there may be…

I understand there are many…

I am convinced the world needs…

I hope to make a small difference in…

Inspired by You

Set up your mat space.

Create an ambiance, just for you—perfect for you right now and this space.

Once your feet are on your mat, close your eyes.

Allow a practice to present itself.

After, if you desire, capture or release.

Carry on.

All your yoga trainings, continuing education, class designs and teaching experiences ultimately enhance your understanding of yoga and your yoga practice.

It is a gift the continually gives.

As long as you are open to receiving.

Remember...

*The biggest adventure you can ever take
is to live the life of your dreams.*

OPRAH WINFREY

Never underestimate the power of your dreams.

Take time to sift through the layers of potential and then find layers of support.

Never underestimate the power of love, it defines:

- Who you are.

- What you do.

- Who embraces you every step along the path.

I have been most fortunate to receive the loving embraces from my spouse, my son, my daughter-in-law, my grandson, my friends, my colleagues and so many others I have met along the way.

Never underestimate the practice of gratitude: for what has been, what is and what will be.

The celebrations.

The challenges.

And everything in-between!

No mud.
No lotus.

THICH NHAT HANH

In good company

Writing is tricky business.

Sometimes the writer thinks good ideas are worthless; other times the writer finds a gem buried beneath a poor idea.

To have a trustworthy companion on the writing journey has more value than what can be put into words.

I have such a companion, always championing my successes, however insignificant.

JR, I simply could not do this without you!

About the Author

Heather is one of millions of nobody famous teachers building a life, a community and a business with her love of teaching and passion for being well in body, mind and spirit.

She applauds those who do the same: yesterday, today and tomorrow.

Together, we make a difference.

www.ingramcontent.com/pod-product-compliance
Lightning Source LLC
Chambersburg PA
CBHW051537020426
42333CB00016B/1974